M

Bloom's Literary Places

DUBLIN
LONDON
NEW YORK
PARIS
ROME
ST. PETERSBURG

Map of St. Petersburg from John Murry's *Handbook for Travellers in Russia, Poland, and Finland* (1893).

Bloom's Literary Places

ST. PETERSBURG

Bradley D. Woodworth and Constance E. Richards

Introduction by
Harold Bloom

CHELSEA HOUSE
PUBLISHERS
A Haights Cross Communications Company
Philadelphia

CHELSEA HOUSE PUBLISHERS
VP, NEW PRODUCT DEVELOPMENT Sally Cheney
DIRECTOR OF PRODUCTION Kim Shinners
CREATIVE MANAGER Takeshi Takahashi
MANUFACTURING MANAGER Diann Grasse

BLOOM'S LITERARY PLACES
EXECUTIVE EDITOR Matt Uhler
EDITORIAL ASSISTANT Sarah Sharpless
SERIES AND COVER DESIGNER Takeshi Takahashi
PHOTO EDITOR Sarah Bloom
LAYOUT EJB Publishing Services

A Haights Cross Communications ⋖ Company

http://www.chelseahouse.com

First Printing

9 8 7 6 5 4 3 2 1

Library of Congress Cataloging-in-Publication Data
Woodworth, Bradley, 1963-
  St. Petersburg / Bradley Woodworth and Constance Richards.
    p. cm. — (Bloom's literary places)
  Includes bibliographical references and index.
  ISBN 0-7910-7837-X (hardcover : alk. paper) 1. Literary landmarks—
Russia (Federation)—Saint Petersburg. 2. Russian literature—History
and criticism. 3. Authors, Russian—Homes and haunts—Russia (Feder-
ation)—Saint Petersburg. 4. Saint Petersburg (Russia)—Intellectual life.
5. Saint Petersburg (Russia)—In literature. I. Title: Saint Petersburg. II.
Richards, Constance, 1967- III. Title. IV. Series.
  PG2996.W66 2005
  891.709'94721—dc22
                                         2005015430

TABLE OF CONTENTS ⬤

Cities of the Mind

It could be argued that the ancestral city for the Western literary imagination is neither Athens nor Jerusalem, but ancient Alexandria, where Hellenism and Hebraism fused and were harvested. All Western writers of authentic aesthetic eminence are Alexandrians, whether they know it or not. Proust and Joyce, Flaubert and Goethe, Shakespeare and Dante rather uneasily share in that eclectic heritage. From the mid-third century before the Common Era through the mid third century after, Alexandria was the city of the spirit and mind and where Plato and Moses did not reconcile (which would be impossible) but abrasively stimulated a new kind of sensibility that we have learned to call Modernism, now twenty-six centuries old. The first Modernist was the poet Callimachus, who said that a long poem was a long evil, and together with his colleagues were approvingly named as *neoteroi* (modernists) by Aristarchus, the earliest literary critic to attempt making a secular canon. Dr. Samuel Johnson, Boileau, Sainte-Beuve, Lessing, Coleridge, I.A. Richards, Empson, and Kenneth Burke are descendants of Aristarchus.

F.E. Peters, in his lucid *The Harvest of Hellenism*, summarizes

the achievement of Hellenistic Alexandria by an impressive cat-
alog: "Gnosticism, the university, the catechetical school, pastoral poetry, monasticism, the romance, grammar, lexicography,
city planning, theology, canon law, heresy and scholasticism." I
don't know why Peters omitted neo-Platonism, inaugurated by
Plotinius, and I myself already have added literary criticism, and
further would list the library. Alexandria has now exiled its
Greeks, Jews, and mostly everyone else not an Arab, and so it is
no longer the city of the mind, and of the poetic tradition that
went the long span from Callimachus to Cavafy. Yet we cannot
arrive at a true appreciation of literary places unless we begin
with Alexandria. I recommend the novelist E.M. Forster's guide
to the city, which deeply ponders its cultural significance.

We are all Alexandrians, as even Dante was, since he
depended upon Hellenistic Neo-Platonic interpretations of
Homer, whose poetry he had never read. Virgil, Dante's guide,
was Hellenistic in culture, and followed Theocritus in pastoral
and Alexandrian imitations of Homer in epic. But though our
literary culture remains Alexandrian (consider all our ongoing
myths of Modernism), we follow St. Augustine in seeing
Jerusalem as the City of God, of King David and his martyred
descendant Jesus of Nazareth. Our universities, inescapably
Alexandrian in their pragmatic eclecticism, nevertheless con-
tinue to exalt the Athens of Socrates, Plato, and Aristotle as the
city of cognition and of (supposed) democracy. The actual Peri-
clean Athens was a slave-owning oligarchy and plutocracy,
which still prevails in much of the world, be it Saudia Arabia or
many of the Americas. Literary Athens, in its Golden Age, built
on Homer and produced the only Western drama that can chal-
lenge Shakespeare: Aeschylus, Euripides, Sophocles, and the
divine Aristophanes (I follow Heinrich Heine who observed
that: "There is a God and his name is Aristophanes").

Athens now slumbers except for Olympic games and
tourism, while Jerusalem is all too lively as the center of Israeli-
Arab contention. Alas, their literary glories have waned, but so
have those of Rome, where Virgil and even the Florentine

Dante are little read or emulated. Cities of the mind are still represented by Paris and London, both perhaps at this moment in cognitive decline. The international language is now American English, and New York City is therefore the literary place-of-places. That, of necessity, has mixed consequences, but those sharpen my renewed comparison to ancient Alexandria, which mingled inventiveness with high decadence, at the end of an age. Alexandria was consciously belated and so are we, despite our paradoxical ecstasy of the new.

2

Is a literary place, by pragmatic definition, a city? Pastoral, like all other literary forms, was an urban invention. The Hebrew Bible, redacted in Babylonian exile, has as its core in Genesis, Exodus, and Numbers, the Yahwist's narrative composed at Solomon's highly sophisticated court in Jerusalem. We cannot locate the inception of what became *Iliad* and *Odyssey*, but the Greece they taught centered at Athens and Thebes. Florence exiled Dante and Cavalcanti, yet shared all further vernacular literary development with Rome and Milan. If Montaigne tended to isolate himself from embattled Paris, he knew his readers remained there. Elizabethan-Jacobean literature is virtually all fixated upon London, and centers upon Shakespeare's Globe Theater. If the American Renaissance emanates out of the Concord of Emerson, Thoreau, Hawthorne, it is equally at home in the New York City of Whitman, Melville, and the burgeoning James family. Though Faulkner kept, as much as he could, to Oxford, Mississippi, and Wallace Stevens to Hartford, if I had to nominate the ultimate classic of the United States in the 20th century, unhesitatingly I would choose the poetry of Hart Crane, Whitman's legitimate heir as the bard of New York City. Kenneth Burke, whenever I saw him from 1975 on, would assure me again that Whitman's "Crossing Brooklyn Ferry" and Hart Crane's *The Bridge* were the two greatest American poems.

Our best living novelists—Philip Roth, Pynchon, DeLillo—

have become inseparable from the ethos of New York City. Only the elusive Cormac McCarthy, seer of *Blood Meridian*, keeps far away from the city-of-cities, which has displaced London and Paris as the world's imaginative capital.

3

However solitary a major writer is by vocation, he or she tends to find a closest friend in a contemporary literary artist. Perhaps rivals attract: Shakespeare and Ben Jonson, Byron and Shelley, Hawthorne and Melville, Hemingway and Scott Fitzgerald, Eliot and Pound, Hart Crane and Allen Tate are just a few pairings, to stay within Anglo-American tradition. Yet the tendency is everywhere: Goethe and Schiller, Wordsworth and Coleridge, Swift and Pope, Tolstoy and Chekhov, Henry James and Edith Wharton, and many more, too numerous to list. The locales waver: Hemingway and Fitzgerald in Paris, Byron and Shelley in Italian exile together, Eliot and Pound in London. There are giant exceptions: Cervantes, Milton, Victor Hugo, Emily Dickinson, Joyce, and Beckett (though only after their early association).

Cities are the essential requisite for literary relationships, including those dominated by a father-figure, the London assemblage of the Sons of Ben Jonson: Carew, Lovelace, Herrick, Suckling, Randoph and many more, or Dr. Samuel Johnson and his club of Boswell, Goldsmith, Burke, among others, or Mallarmé and his disciples, including Valéry, who was to surpass his master. Modernist London always calls up Bloomsbury, with Virginia Woolf as its luminous figure, the ornament of a group that in its own idiosyncratic mode saw E.M. Forster as its patriarch.

Even in the age of the computer screen, proximity is essential for literary fellowship. But so far I have considered the city as literary place only in regard to writers. As subject, indeed as *the given* of literature, the city is a larger matter. The movement from garden to city as literary focus is powerfully clear in the Hebrew Bible, when Yahweh moves his abode from Mount

Sinai to Mount Zion, and thus to Solomon's Temple. As the mountain of the Covenant, Sinai stands at the origin, but surprisingly Ezekiel (28:13 following) locates "Eden, the garden of God" as a plateau on Zion, both cosmological mountain and paradise. When Yahweh takes up residence in the Temple, his Eden is close by, yet nevertheless the transition from garden to city has been accomplished. This is the Holy City, but to the literary imagination all the great cities are sacred: Paris, London, Dublin, Petersburg, Rome, and New York are also sanctified, whatever suffering and inequity transpire in them.

4

In the United States the national capital, Washington D.C., is scarcely a city of the mind, not only when contrasted to New York City, but also to Boston, Chicago, San Francisco. Paris, London, and Rome are at once capitals and literary centers, but Washington D.C. has harbored few major American writers and has provided subjects only for political novelists, like Henry Adams and Gore Vidal. The Great American Novel perpetually remains to be written, despite such earlier splendors as *The Scarlet Letter*, *Moby-Dick*, *Huckleberry Finn*, and *The Portrait of a Lady*, and a handful of later masterpieces from *As I Lay Dying* and *The Sound and the Fury*, *The Sun Also Rises* and *The Great Gatsby*, on to *Gravity's Rainbow*, *Sabbath's Theater*, *Underworld*, and *Blood Meridian*. I rather doubt that it will take Washington, D.C. as subject, or be composed by an inhabitant thereof.

The industrialization of the great cities in the nineteenth century gave us the novels of Victor Hugo, Dickens, Zola which produced a realism totally phantasmagoric, now probably no longer available to us. Computer urbanism does not seem likely to stimulate imaginative literature. Visual overdetermination overwhelms the inward eye and abandons us to narrative or the formal splendors of poetry and drama. There is something hauntingly elegiac about fresh evocations of literary places, here and now in the early years of the 21st century.

HAROLD **BLOOM**

Introduction

Pushkin forever will be the poet of St. Petersburg, even as Gogol will be its mad tale-teller, and Dostoevsky the city's visionary novelist. Never having gone to Russia, from which my father migrated, I have no personal experience of St. Petersburg. Since I approach seventy-five, I am not likely ever to see the perpetual literary center of Russia, Moscow's ongoing rival in that country's cultural life.

The more-than-Byronic Pushkin created a masterpiece in his great poem, *The Bronze Horseman*, which continues to influence Russian poetry. But here I wish to emphasize the phantasmagorias of Gogol and of Dostoevsky, because these have characterized St. Petersburg as emphatically as Charles Dickens's grotesque splendors have captured every fog that rolls through London.

Gogol was a sublime madman, in life and in art, imperishably portrayed in the wonderful short story, "Gogol's Wife," by Tommaso Landolfi, the precursor of Italo Calvino in modern Italian fiction. In Gogol's St. Petersburg, anything and everything can and does happen. Freud remarked that there are no accidents, but in Gogol there is nothing else. Even what cannot happen anywhere else takes place in Gogolian Petersburg, where you can find a human nose lurking in your morning bread.

Nabokov accurately saluted Gogol as his forerunner, and the spirit of Gogol (to call it that) lives on in Nabokov's masterwork, *Pale Fire*. No one, Nabokov included, surpasses Gogol in his peculiar mode of realistic fantasy. Whenever something dreadfully unexpected, and unmerited, breaks into my life, I reluctantly think of Gogol. To read his Petersburg stories is a delight, but to live them is quite another experience.

The eminence of Pushkin, and of Gogol, never can be set aside, but the literary seer of St. Petersburg finally has to be Dostoevsky, whose *Crime and Punishment* always will remain the definitive nightmare of the city. Raskolnikov, Svidrigailov, and Porfiry play out their drama in a nightmare metropolis that gives off a sinister yellow sheen. In that decaying atmosphere, Raskolnikov gratuitously slaughters two old women, in an attempt to persuade himself he is a Napoleon of negation. Porfiry, endlessly shrewd police inspector, performs his slow dance around Raskolnikov, while assuring the wretched student that: "You can't do without me." The book's greatest creation, the nihilist Svidrigailov, assures us that eternity is a filthy bathhouse in the country, seething with spiders. As he commits suicide, by shooting himself, Svidrigailov zestfully answers a policeman's query as to what he is doing: "Going to America!" Perhaps that is the single moment that sums up the aesthetic power, and the destructive principle, of literary St. Petersburg.

CHAPTER ONE

St. Petersburg Today

Short, dark winter days; long "white" summer nights—St. Petersburg's contradictions serve the soul of a writer well. The city along the wide Neva River is at once achingly beautiful and inconsolably dreary. Constructed on a swamp in Russia's cold North, the city boasts magnificent baroque and rococo-style structures in the pastel hues of Easter basket confections, as well as a network of canals and bridges that prompt its nickname of "Venice of the North." These grand concepts were imported by Peter the Great, inspired by the architectural flair of Venice or Versailles and other European metropoli, in his quest to create St. Petersburg as Russia's "Window on the West" at the dawn of the 18th century.

The capital of imperial Russia, an empire spanning Europe and Asia, St. Petersburg boasted architecture, administration, social life, and even language (the court's French) that were influenced by other cultures, so much so that it would be called Russia's most European city. But this, coupled with the city's very Russian winter and Russian inhabitants, many of them descendents of the workers Peter herded into the city to build it, makes for a place of uncommon contrast and mystery.

Palaces and ornate mansions line bridge-covered canals, giving the city a dramatic glow at every angle ... from every view, even on the dreary days that make up much of the area's climate.

A network of 500 bridges, from small foot bridges to multi-laned thoroughfares, crisscrosses the waters of the magical city, linking museums like the grand Hermitage to the famed St. Petersburg Academy of Arts or the Peter and Paul Fortress to the rest of the city, not to mention connecting the quieter residential neighborhoods to bustling Nevsky Prospekt.

Russia's "city of culture," spawned some of the country's greatest writers, composers, artists, and dancers. Today, over 50 museums lie within the city limits. The Kirov Ballet, now reverted to its pre-revolutionary name of Mariinsky, is known the world over. The Hermitage Museum rivals the Louvre.

Palaces and estates dot the countryside around the city, having served as prime real estate for Russian royalty. Yet tragedy would befall those grand places, not only when many buildings were indiscriminately pressed into service as military academies, factories, prisons, clinics, communal living quarters, and allowed to crumble into decay under the Soviet regime, but also when world war came to Russia and Nazi troops plundered the historical structures ... forever losing the Catherine Palace's Amber Room, for example.

Decades of revolutionary fervor finally erupted in the early 1900s, bringing the Romanov dynasty to an end, and moving power back to Moscow under the new regime of the Soviets.

Though never invaded by hostile forces, St. Petersburg, then called Leningrad, endured the 900-day siege in World War Two. The city, with a great loss of many residents to cold and starvation, survived nearly three years of attacks. Even in over 70 years of the Socialist regime, St. Petersburg was able to keep its individuality with precious little imposing Soviet architecture dominating the city landscape—allowing the legacy of an imperial capital of 200 years to remain largely intact.

Today St. Petersburg is a city of beauty, elegance, and grandeur, that thrives on tourism and its reputation of intellectualism and culture. The White Nights in June see visitors from all over the world flocking to the city's classical music and performance festivals. But in its decline in the post-Soviet decade leading into the 21st century, St. Petersburg became a sad grande dame, whose crumbling façades and potholed streets had seen better days ... better centuries.

Fortunately, St. Petersburg enjoys glory days once again, albeit in fits and quivers—in part to the facelift it received celebrating its 300th birthday in 2003, its fame as birthplace of Russian President Vladimir Putin, and to investment by new industry.

While St. Petersburg has nowhere reached the proportions of the foreign and domestic investment of Moscow, which boasts construction at near lightning speed, futuristic advertising billboards on every corner, and shopping excess on a grand scale, St. Petersburg is the genteel ballerina to Moscow's brash chorus girl—always classy and steeped in the culture of poetic history.

A QUICK EVOLUTION

Peter the Great's efforts to create a new imperial capital from the ground up were greatly successful after he trounced the Swedes who were encroaching on Russia's north at the vast Neva River. Peter established the Peter and Paul Fortress on the waters a few miles in from the sea in 1703. Following Holland's example, Peter dug canals to drain the marshy land that was situated at sea level. He imported engineers from the Netherlands, architects from Italy, and residents from the rest of Russia to establish what would become the country's new capital in 1712.

Besides peasants from the countryside who would become forced laborers to build the city, he brought in administrators, noblemen, and merchants to populate the emerging city. St. Petersburg grew exponentially from nothing in only a few decades. By Peter's death in 1725, most of Russia's foreign trade was passing through the city's ports. Trade, shipbuilding, and Peter's naval regiments and academies flourished.

Catherine the Great, married to Peter's grandson Peter III, ascended to the throne when she deposed of the despised Peter III in a coup d'etat in 1762. He was eventually murdered by Catherine's lover Orlov. Pursued by innuendo and rumor all her life, Catherine nonetheless cultivated a St. Petersburg blossoming in the arts and sciences. Her royal art collection would be the nucleus for the Hermitage Museum.

She also oversaw the creation of new buildings for the Russian Academy of Sciences, the Academy of Fine Arts (Catherine's aunt, by marriage, Elizabeth I founded the Academy) and the first Public Library (now the Russian National Library).

Years of growth in mercantile and industry followed.

During World War One the city cast off its German-sounding name and became Petrograd.

But the looming political and economic crisis of the Russian Empire grew, and in the fall of 1917 the Bolshevik party, led by Vladimir Lenin, gained political power. On November 7, 1917, a shot ringing out from the battleship Aurora gave the signal to the waiting workers and soldiers to storm the Winter Palace, the current residence of the Provisional Government that came after the deposing of Tsar Nicholas II. Thus began a civil war that eventually resulted in the Bolsheviks spreading communist rule over all Russia and the formation of the Soviet Union.

In the meantime German troops were so close to Petrograd in 1918 that the Bolshevik government moved the capital to Moscow. In 1924 the name of the city was changed to Leningrad in honor of Vladimir Ilych Lenin.

The city suffered the loss of a great many lives during the 900-day Siege of Leningrad in World War Two.

Finally, in 1991—the year that Communism in the Soviet Union fell and peaceful protests by millions of residents on Palace Square took place—residents voted on changing the city's name back to St. Petersburg in a democratic referendum.

A CITY BESIEGED

As pre-revolutionary as the city seems with its chiefly imperial architecture, the ravages of the worst of the 20th century weighed heavily on this place. St. Petersburg, Petrograd, Leningrad—as the political changes warranted various names—experienced some of the darkest days of war during the Siege of Leningrad in World War Two.

The Second World War claimed over 20 million Soviet lives. Some of the fiercest fighting took place around St. Petersburg, then called Leningrad, when the Nazis kept the city under siege for 900 days. Hundreds of thousands of people died in the city (mostly of cold and starvation). People aged 20 years in those three, proof of which lies in scores of documentary photographs in Russia's Red Army archives in Podolsk, outside Moscow, opened to the public for the first time in 1991.

Over 600,000 residents died during the time of the siege, of which at least 420,000 were civilians. They are buried in the city's Piskariovskoye Cemetery in 186 mass graves.

An impressive monument to the city's survival of the siege stands on the road to the international Pulkovo Airport. Built in the shape of a large broken ring that symbolizes the efforts to break the siege, the monument is the focus of Ploshchad Pobedy (Victory Square).

CITY OF MUSEUMS

Even during Soviet times, St. Petersburg was known as the cultural capital of Russia—boasting theater, ballet, and art museums of great renown. The Hermitage Museum, on par with Paris's Louvre, and the Mariinsky Ballet (often known by the old name of Kirov), for example, have maintained Russia's reputation as a fruitful cultivator of the arts. Over fifty museums, numerous monuments and sculptures make up the city's cultural framework. Parks and walkable green spaces abound.

Great artists of the ages like Repin, Nesterov, Roerikh, Savrasov, Surikov, and Brodsky, studied at the Academy of Arts, founded by Elizabeth I, on the banks of the Neva.

Many palaces, most of them created in the 18th century in the styles of rococo, baroque, then neoclassical, have been turned into museums, showcasing much of Russia's imperial grandeur in splendid collections of icons, jewels, paintings, and sculptures.

White Nights

From late May to early July, St. Petersburg's nights are barely discernible from its days—with only a smidgen of graying skies during the summer solstice of June 21. Located 59 degrees 57' North (about the same latitude as the southern tip of Greenland), St. Petersburg is one of the few urban centers to experience the White Nights of summer. The exact opposite of its winter, where night seems to take over the day, leaving precious few light hours in the dreary winter. The romantic White Nights create a type of mania among the city's inhabitants.

St. Petersburgers make the most of their bright summer with all-night walks along the canals of the city. A splashy well-orchestrated White Nights Festival of classical music, opera, and dance around the city attracts tourists. Street performers entertain late-night strollers, and wandering musicians gather groups of friends on the banks of the Neva for sing-alongs.

The sun shines in golden strata over the banks of Vasilievsky Island toward midnight, and only then releases its grip on the city, relinquishing a few hours to dusk. While St. Petersburg isn't the only city far enough north to experience a sun that doesn't set, it is the world's most northern city with a population of over 3 million to claim the White Nights.

But stay out too late and you chance being left on the wrong side of the Neva, depending on where you're headed. The drawbridges go up like clockwork on a rotating timeline, allowing for ships and barges to pass through on their journey in and out of St. Petersburg's port and to the rest of Russia.

Just outside St. Petersburg, the palaces have become show-pieces of Russia's Romanov Dynasty—Peterhof, Peter the Great's summer palace some 20 miles outside the city, with its marvelous gardens and trick fountains that surprise unlucky passersby with an impromptu squirt of water; the Catherine Palace in Pushkin, named for Peter's wife Catherine I, no longer with with its Amber Room that disappeared forever after being plundered by the Nazis; Oranienbaum, also known as Lomonosov; Pavlovsk, the palace Catherine the Great awarded her son Paul; and others.

RESIDENTS OF A CULTURAL CAPITAL

Stereotypes of St. Petersburg residents abound—alternately called cool and aloof, or elegant and reserved, the residents pride themselves in their cultured past and in their progressive present. Considered more "European" than their brethren in cities to the south and the east during the Soviet era, St. Peters-burgers (or Leningraders as they were then known), often had easier access to foreigners coming to Russia as tourists or students. Being so close to Scandinavia, the city was often a weekend sojourn for Finns or Swedes on holiday ... particularly when vodka prices were exceptionally low, compared to the rates of alcohol at home.

The city was also close to the Baltic states, where the standard of living was high and influence from the outside the USSR more abundant. Students of Russian language venturing behind the Iron Curtain often preferred picturesque Leningrad, with a simmering underground scene of music and art, to dour and gray Moscow. An energetic and youthful trade of ideas fed on the eclecticism of old St. Petersburg charm and intelligentsia, mingled with the embracing of things modern and avant-garde.

Poet Anna Akhmatova railed against Soviet oppression and though silenced for a time, remained one of the fiercest symbols of St. Petersburg's significant intelligentsia.

The mania of a city that never sleeps in the summer—

celebrating the White Nights with all-night music festivals; wandering guitar-strumming minstrels along the Neva; groups of youths waiting for the drawbridges to lower so they can get home again—is never quite forgotten, even during the shortest days of winter, when depressive darkness and cold keeps residents hibernating indoors until the next cycle of midnight sun begins again.

CITY OF ART AND MUSIC

Casinos, giant department stores, nightclubs, and famous restaurants en masse may be missing from this literary capital, still on the road to self-realization in capitalist Russia. Instead, one finds dramatic theater, ballet, bookshops, and open-air art markets in many a neighborhood.

The Hermitage Museum, once neglected and suffering structural damage under Soviet economic hardships, has entered a new era of benefaction and world class exhibitions.

The State Russian Museum, with the finest collection of Russian art from Repin to Vrubel, and now beyond—with a new modern and pop art wing—inspires lovers of quintessential Russian art.

The Mariinsky (Kirov) Theater of Opera and Ballet has inspired poets, writers, artists, and dancers themselves, to leap into the genre of the classical "ballet Russes," having given rise to such greats as Diaghilev, Petipa, Nijinksy, Pavlova, Nureyev, Baryshnikov, and others.

Promoted as the progressive capital of Russia by Peter the Great, much of the city's forward-thinking philosophy resonated with the avant-garde of later centuries, as well as in more recent times—with artists' movements such Pushkinskaya 10, a conglomerate of contemporary once-underground artists that began in squatters' flats on Pushkin Street 10. Today it is an art center with studios for experimental art, music, and an exhibition hall.

Another group of young artists emerging in the early 1990s created the New Academy of Arts, known for its radical interpretations of Russian avant-garde and neo-expressionism.

Many of the founding members have gone on to exhibit around the world, including at New York's MOMA.

Russia's first electronic music-fueled raves took place in squatters' apartments on the Fontanka canal, the planetarium, and the grounds of the Artillery Museum, located in the crown-work of the Peter and Paul Fortress—small, modern-day under-ground revolutions when they occurred for the first time in the Soviet Union of the late '80s and early '90s.

INTELLECTUAL CAPITAL

Though no longer the political capital of Russia, St. Petersburg is the second largest city in Russia, with over 4 million residents, and will forever remain its intellectual capital. Current Russian President Vladimir Putin, who hails from Petersburg, has culled from the city's local government and brought many civil leaders to serve in his government at the Kremlin.

While that has boosted the city's political standing within the Russian Federation, it has also depleted St. Petersburg of resi-dents (politicians' families follow them to Moscow). Others have moved to Moscow to pursue business and investment opportunities that come more slowly to quiet St. Petersburg. As a result, the population of the city on the Neva has fallen dra-matically in the past ten years.

Often, in the words of native sons like Nikolai Gogol, Fyodor Dostoevsky, (and with a bit of humor) Mikhail Zoshchenko ... the city comes across as a dank, dark, vapid place, with dark hallways in low-slung buildings slowly descending into the bog on which it was built, the constant damp and chill mildewing a soul from within.

Short winter days, where "light" is only gray imitation of day for a few hours at best, haunt the pages of Russian literature.

But in reality, St. Petersburg's narrow alleyways and oppres-sive courtyards are countered by the sweeping vistas of Palace Square before the grand Winter Palace, the vastness of the Neva as it flows into the Bay of Finland, the poetic, cobblestoned palazzos of the magnificent Peter and Paul Fortress.

St. Petersburg is simply a city bound to elicit the purest of emotions, inspire the most contradictory of feelings, and remain in the hearts of those who visit it forever.

CHAPTER TWO

Foundation
for a New Russia

*"The founding of St. Petersburg is the greatest proof of that
ardor of the Russian will which does not know anything
is impossible." —Madame de Staël*

Saint Petersburg was born first as an idea in the mind of
Russia's Tsar Peter the Great. Rising out of an inhospitable
marshland to become one of the world's most vibrant and beautiful cities, St. Petersburg is a testament to the imagination and
willpower of Peter the Great. For Peter, this new city embodied
his vision for Russia's future as a power spanning East and West.
The realization of Peter's vision and the city's continuing growth
and success in the three centuries since its founding are remarkable achievements.

St. Petersburg was founded in the Neva River delta, in a
region known as Ingermanland, or Ingria (also Izhorskaya
Zemlya). The region around the Gulf of Finland, where St.
Petersburg lies today, was first settled in the 8th or 9th century
A.D. and populated by various ethnic groups, including Slavs
and Finns, among others. While the swampy land itself was not
ideal for fishing or farming, its location on the Baltic Sea made

it a key point of trade between East and West, and the object of much territorial dispute over the centuries. The principality of Novgorod, later subdued by Russia, claimed the area in the 10th century. In 1240, the Swedes launched an invasion on the banks of the Neva, but Prince Alexander Nevsky of Novgorod, who was later made a saint by the Russian Orthodox Church for his valiant protection of Russia, defeated the Swedes on July 15, 1240 in the Battle of Neva. Under the control of Novgorod the region passed into the hands of the royal family of Moscow. After the death of Tsar Fiodor Ioanovich, son of Ivan the Terrible and last of the Riurik dynasty, Vasily Shuisky came to power. Shuisky approached the Swedes as potential allies, but sensing Russia's weakness, the Swedes instead reclaimed the region in the 1617 Stolbovo Treaty, wresting control of the Baltic trade routes away from the Russians.

PETER'S GRAND VISION

When Peter the Great assumed power at the end of the 17th century, he envisioned a new Russia that would rival the major European powers. He saw the region around the Neva River as a strategic location on the Baltic Sea from which to develop Russia's commercial and political relationship with Europe. Under Peter's direction, Russia retook control of the region during the Second (Great) Northern War (1700–1721). His general, Alexander Danilovich Menshikov, who would later become the first governor of St. Petersburg, defeated the Swedes at the fortress of Nyenskans in 1703 and regained control over the Neva River.

The city, established upon a network of islands within the Neva delta, was founded on Zayachy Island (the "Isle of Hares") (Lincoln 17) on May 16, 1703 (May 27 according to the modern calendar). Several legends tell of the founding of St. Petersburg. Pushkin himself immortalized the event at the beginning of his poem *The Bronze Horseman*, imagining Peter standing "On the shore of empty waves [...] filled with great thoughts, and star[ing] out" (Volkov, *St. Petersburg: A Cultural*

History 6). Another legend echoes the founding of Constantinople, telling of Peter sighting an eagle overhead and choosing to found the city on that spot (6). Yet another legend has Peter marking the spot with crucifixes, declaring that he would build a church there to honor Saints Peter and Paul, and then beginning the labor with his own hands.

However, despite these legends, historians surmise that Peter was probably not even on Zayachy Island on the day of its founding—May 16, 1703. It was rather General Menshikov who, after defeating the Swedes at the fortress of Nyenskans, laid the groundwork on the uninhabitable swampland that was Zayachy (Volkov 6), naming it Sankt Pieter Burkh in honor of Peter's patron saint.

The island, which would later become the Fortress of Saints Peter and Paul, and the surrounding region were a far from ideal site for the founding of a city; the area was marshland prone to flooding and lacking a reliable source of fresh water or timber. But Peter's ambitions extended far beyond these impediments. Having traveled in Europe in his youth, Peter was inspired by the cities there—particularly Amsterdam. He was fascinated by the modern, comfortable lifestyle of Europeans, which was far superior to that of the Russians, and he hoped that Russia could emulate Holland's successful seafaring industry.

Peter is often said to have seen St. Petersburg as his "window on Europe," but those are the words not of the Tsar himself but of Count Francesco Algarotti, an Italian traveler writing in his *Lettera sulla Russia* (1739) (Volkov, *St. Petersburg* 10). In his own words, Peter described St. Petersburg as his "new Rome," his "paradise" or "promised land" (Lincoln 21). Wishing to relocate Russia's spiritual center from Moscow to St. Petersburg, he identified the city as the New Jerusalem described in the Book of Revelation. Everything about the new city would contrast with Moscow: St. Petersburg represented European Russia, modernization, and secularization, while Moscow represented Asiatic Russia, the past, and the domination of Church over State.

SOMETHING OUT OF NOTHING

Shortly after the city's founding, its first house was built of logs. Peter himself stayed there and had it painted to look like the brick houses he had seen in Amsterdam. Today it is

Kunstkammer

Peter the Great was not only fascinated by ships, canals, architecture, and artillery, but also by the world's peoples and nature's oddities. Considered one of the world's oldest ethnographic museums, St. Petersburg's Kunstkammer on Vasilievsky Island began as Peter's personal collection of ethnographic and archaeological objects.

Peter I opened the museum by decree in 1714 in the Summer Palace, later moving it to the magnificent baroque building it still inhabits today. In 1724 the Kunstkammer (which literally means "art chamber" in German), was given to the St. Petersburg Academy of Sciences.

The museum's ethnographic, anthropological and archaeological collections reflect the culture and everyday life of many of the world's peoples. It houses an early anatomical collection purchased from a Dutch anatomist in 1717. Artifacts from early Siberian, Antarctic, and Kamchatka (Russia's far eastern peninsula) explorations contributed to the exhibition hall, as well as explorations by Russia's scholars farther abroad to New Guinea, Polynesia, and other corners of the world.

Most unusual, however, is Peter's personal collection of curiosities that could rival a Ripley's Believe It or Not. One chamber is devoted to those oddities—large jars containing a variety of "monsters of nature"—diseased organs; grossly deformed animal fetuses, some with two heads; and a variety of human fetuses.

preserved as a museum and called "The Cabin of Peter the Great." In 1704, Peter erected the Fortress of Saints Peter and Paul. After the victory over the Swedes at Poltava in 1709, a small palace was built for Peter and his second wife, Catherine. The first stone palace, built in 1714 for Menshikov, is also preserved today. Peter later commissioned both a Summer and a Winter Palace for himself.

Peter initially wanted the city's center to be in the area between the fortress and his cabin, an area that later came to be called Trinity Square after the city's first church, Trinity Cathedral. Contrary to his wishes, however, the true center of St. Petersburg naturally developed on the opposite side of the Neva around the Admiralty shipyard where the Russian fleet was built. This part of the city came to house many important institutions during the century after the city's founding, including the Winter Palace, the Holy Synod, St. Isaac's Cathedral, and the Imperial Ruling Senate (Lincoln 19). Until bridges were constructed, people had to cross the river in ferries, thus inspiring St. Petersburg's nickname "the Venice of the North."

Envisioning a grand, spacious, orderly city with the Admiralty at its center, Peter brought architects and craftsmen from around Russia and the world to participate in the creation of the city's squares, canals, and boulevards. The city was organized geometrically along *pershpektivy* or prospects, the longest and most important of which was Nevsky Prospect, designed by the French architect Jean-Baptiste Le Blond and built in 1715 (Volkov, *St. Petersburg* 11). Peter also relied heavily on the services of the Italian-Swiss architect Domenico Trezzini, who based the initial designs for the city on a Northern European Protestant style inspired by Amsterdam. In 1706, Peter commissioned Trezzini to expand the Fortress of Saints Peter and Paul and to build the cathedral there; Peter would later be buried at this cathedral, as was much of the rest of the Romanov family. He had Trezzini construct a second Winter Palace on the Neva River and the St. Alexander Nevsky monastery at the end of Nevsky Prospect.

The city was built by forced labor, and the marshy environs of its foundation resulted in the deaths of many of the laborers who worked to build it. The 19th century historian V.O. Kliuchevskii called St. Petersburg "a huge graveyard" and claimed that its creation was as deadly as any battle (Lincoln 21). Tens of thousands of peasants from across Russia were forced to travel across Russia to the site, and while many managed to escape en route, those who did not escape likely died from privation, illness, or exhaustion. In order to establish the presence of the middle and upper classes in the city, Peter also forced noblemen and merchants to relocate to St. Petersburg and build their own homes according to a strictly prescribed style designed by architect Domenico Trezzini. Built and populated by the sheer force of Peter's will and ambition, St. Petersburg was the object of both imperial propaganda and popular hostility. One legend tells of Peter's first wife Eudoxia, who was later sent to a convent, cursing the city with the words "Sankt-Peterburg will stand empty" (Volkov, *St. Petersburg* 14). Another legend told of the kikimora, a monster who inhabited the bell tower of Trinity Church, foretelling the doom of the city by flood (14)— a not entirely unlikely scenario, given the region's vulnerability to flooding.

THE NEW POLITICAL AND CULTURAL CAPITAL

In 1712, St. Petersburg became the capital of Russia, even though Sweden did not formally surrender power until the Peace of Nystad in 1721. Growth was rapid; early buildings included the Merchant's Exchange (today the Naval Museum), the Customs House (today the Museum of Literature), the Summer Palace, and the marine hospital.

As a result of Peter's efforts to direct commerce and exchange toward the new city, St. Petersburg soon became Russia's major port. The Vyshnevolotsky Canal in the Valdai Hills was constructed between 1703 and 1709. St. Petersburg soon became a city of canals and bridges. The growth of the shipbuilding industry, centered at the Admiralty shipyard, was followed by the construction of foundries and factories, and then later, by the century's end, with the development of printing, food, and apparel industries.

Peter's vision of a new Russia included a renovation of its culture as well. St. Petersburg soon became known as a "city of palaces" (Lincoln 25). Among the upper classes, European baroque style dominated not only architecture and furniture but also clothing and entertainment (26). Peter had Le Blond, who had helped design Louis XIV's gardens at Versailles, design the Summer Gardens, which became the setting for the Summer Palace (Lincoln 26–27). Peter supported a number of new writers, including Antioch Kantemir, Vassily Trediakovsky, Mikhail Lomonosov, and Alexander Sumarokov, all of whom lauded and mythologized both Peter and the new city (Volkov, *St. Petersburg* 16). Despite the state-supported propaganda, the founding of the city so quickly and in such an inhospitable setting was certainly a feat.

AFTER PETER THE GREAT

After his death in 1725, Peter was succeeded by his wife, Catherine I, who ruled briefly, until she died in 1727. She was in turn succeeded by their thirteen-year-old grandson Peter II, who moved the capital back to Moscow the following year, prompting many of the aristocrats who had been forced to move to Moscow to follow suit. This resulted in the cultural and political decline of St. Petersburg, although trade remained strong and continued to grow.

After Peter II died of smallpox in 1730, Empress Anna Ivanovna (1730–40) moved the capital back to St. Petersburg, where it remained between 1741 and 1825 during the reigns of Empress Elizabeth, Catherine the Great, and Alexander I. Urban growth and construction began anew, and a national style of architecture developed under the influence of the architects Petr Eropkin, Ivan Korobov, and Mikhail Zemstov (Lincoln 32). After Anna Ivanovna died in 1740, Peter the Great's daughter Elizabeth seized the throne in 1741.

The Bridges of St. Petersburg

Built on the delta of the River Neva, St. Petersburg and its environs spread over a series of large and small islands—one hundred and one in all. The city itself is criss-crossed by a network
of canals and tributaries of the Neva. To maneuver around
St. Petersburg and its many waters, Peter the Great commissioned the building of a number of remarkable bridges. In the
centuries that followed others were added, many becoming
architectural treasures.

The city of St. Petersburg has the largest number of bridges
in the world, even more than Venice. There are 539 bridges
altogether, with over 300 in the downtown area.

The first bridge was built in 1703, the year the city was
founded. It connected the Peter and Paul Fortress with the rest
of the city. The first permanent bridge across the Neva River was
constructed from 1842 to 1850 and anointed the Lieutenant
Schmidt Bridge.

The Alexander Nevsky Bridge, at 2971 feet and five inches, is
the longest, and the Blue Bridge (or Siny Most) is the widest, at
319 feet and two inches in width.

The narrowest bridge of St. Petersburg is also one of the city's
favorites—the charming Bank Bridge that spans the Moika Canal
at a narrow spot. Its golden-winged griffons stand watch over
the bridge, and over a building that formerly served as the city's
central bank. Bank Bridge is just one inch over six feet wide.

Between April and October after the Neva thaws, the bridges
spanning the river are raised at night to let ships pass. Some
Petersburgers who stay out too late find themselves stuck on
the wrong side of the city until morning ... but most of the drawbridges close only after 4:30 A.M.

Wanting to build upon Peter the Great's vision of St. Petersburg, Empress Elizabeth brought the Italian architect Bartolomeo Francesco Rastrelli to St. Petersburg. His works, influenced by the European baroque as well as by his Parisian education and Italian heritage, dominated the construction that took place in St. Petersburg from 1741 to 1761 and defined the flamboyant, rococo-like style of St. Petersburg under Empress Elizabeth (Lincoln 35). One of his first works in St. Petersburg was a mansion commissioned by Prince Dmitri Kantemir, built on the Millionnaia avenue along the Neva River. Rastrelli's other commissions included the "third" Summer Palace, the Peterhof Palace, the Catherine Palace, as well as plans for the Smolnyi Cathedral and Convent, which were not completed until the 1830s. Rastrelli's masterpiece was the expansion of the ornate Winter Palace built on the Neva, begun in 1754 but not completed until 1817, after the deaths of both the Empress and the architect. This "fourth" Winter Palace eventually became the Hermitage Museum.

Empress Elizabeth died in 1761 while occupying a temporary wooden residence Rastrelli had built for her to live in until the completion of the new Winter Palace. Elizabeth was succeeded by Emperor Peter III, who reigned only briefly and took little interest in building up the city (Lincoln 44). The elaborate, baroque style favored by Empress Elizabeth would later be tempered by the neoclassical tastes of Catherine the Great, who came to power in 1762. By the time of Catherine the Great's rule, St. Petersburg had become a cosmopolitan city with vital trade and a population of almost 200,000 (Lincoln 42).

Modeled after the great cities of Europe and conceived in Peter the Great's imagination, St. Petersburg after fewer than sixty years of existence already promised to become a great European capital in its own right—a lasting symbol of Russia's new status in Europe and in the world.

CHAPTER THREE

Pushkin and
"The Bronze Horseman"

The symbolic literary center of Petersburg is without doubt the huge equestrian statue of Peter the Great that stands on Decembrists Square (*ploshchad' Dekabristov*, known in pre-revolutionary Russia as Senate Square, *Senatskaia ploshchad'*). From his perch atop a towering steed, Peter peers northward, across the banks of the Neva River. Behind him looms the dark mass of St. Isaac's Cathedral. This magnificent monument is unofficially, but most commonly, known as the Bronze Horseman (*Mednyi vsadnik*), after the poem by Pushkin. It is the greatest and most famous monument in all of Russia—indeed one of the finest in all of Europe—and is universally seen as a symbol of Russia and its greatness.

Unveiled in 1782, it is the work of Parisian sculptor Etienne-Maurice Falconet. He was commissioned for the task by empress Catherine the Great, who sought by erecting the monument to bask in the reflected grandeur of her illustrious predecessor. Catherine decided upon a monument for Peter in 1764, just two years after her ascension to the throne at the age of thirty-five. Born a German princess—her name before her marriage to the heir to the Russian throne was Sophie Frederike

Auguste von Anhalt-Zerbst. Catherine had become empress after colluding in the murder of her hated Prussophilic husband, the newly-crowned emperor Peter III. Though a grandson of Peter I (the Great), by character Peter III was more German than Russian. Catherine, without a drop of Russian blood, quickly mastered the Russian language, converted to Orthodoxy, and set out to out-Russian the Russians in ruling over her adopted land. Catherine wanted the monument not only to be a material paean to Peter, but a statement about the greatness of

The Winter Palace

The phenomenal green and white structure that now houses the world-renowned Hermitage Museum was once a grand palace built for Empress Elizabeth, the progeny of Peter the Great. Known as the Winter Palace (Zimny Dvorets), the 1,057-room confection is a sample of the gorgeous Baroque style that decorates many of St. Petersburg's institutions and royal palaces. It was conceived by one of the court's favorite architects, Italian Francesco Rastrelli. Built primarily between 1754 and 1762, the palace was eventually completed by Catherine the Great, niece of Elizabeth, after the death of the latter.

A fire in 1837 nearly destroyed the building, but today its ornate rooms and impressive mirrored halls house one of the greatest art collections in the world. The Hermitage collections number over 3 million works of art from the Stone Age to the 20th century. Much of the art was collected by Catherine. The museum houses one of the greatest collections of Western European art in the world, with works from Leonardo da Vinci, Raphael, Caravaggio, Michelangelo, Degas, Manet, Matisse, Picasso, and many more of note.

An extensive collection of Russian religious icons and cultural works makes up another part of the collection, as well as antiquities, Oriental art, and prehistoric art.

the Russian empire. A monument that not only was grandiose but also great art would in addition reflect well on her, she reasoned. It was clear that an artist capable of achieving all these ends would have to come from Western Europe. Catherine was also keen to strengthen her ties with the intellectual and artistic world of the French Enlightenment. Falconet's ties with *philosophes* in Paris thus helped him secure the commission.

FALCONET ARRIVES

The fifty-year-old Falconet came to Petersburg in 1766, accompanied by his eighteen-year-old assistant, Anne-Marie Collot. Work on the monument progressed slowly. The statue was not assembled until more than a decade later—the bronze figure was cast in separate sections because of its great size. The granite boulder that forms the statue's plinth was found near a peasant village some thirteen miles from St. Petersburg. Called "Thunder Rock" by the peasants, the future foundation for the mounted Peter was what geologists call an erratic boulder, and was one of many such large formations left along the shores of the Baltic Sea by retreating sheets of ice at the end of the last Ice Age. The boulder's measurements were staggering: 42 feet long, 27 feet wide, and 21 feet high; it weighed approximately 1,800 metric tons. Trimmed of a third of its original heft to shape it for the needs of the monument, this erratic stone wanderer was pushed, pulled, and floated on barges to its final resting place on Senate Square. Given the technology of 18th-century Russia, this was an awe-inspiring feat of engineering (as it inched along, onlookers called the boulder a "mountain on eggs") that took nearly two years to accomplish.

The completed monument presents Peter dressed in classical robes on a rearing steed, his gaze fixed ahead, right hand extended, as if surveying land he has just conquered. Below the horse's hooves a snake lies trampled. The equestrian Peter stands sixteen and a half feet tall, and the stone foundation is nearly the same height. Falconet added the snake late in the planning process; fearing that the winds that blew across Senate Square might be too much for such a huge statue poised only on the rear legs of the horse, the snake provided a third point of balance. Like the rest of the statue, the meaning of the snake has received various interpretations.

PUSHKIN'S INSPIRATION

The statue is the inspiration for one of the highest achievements in Russian literature, the narrative poem *The Bronze Horseman: A Tale of St. Petersburg*, written in 1833 by Russia's greatest poet, Alexander Pushkin (1799–1837). From the moment of the monument's unveiling, the huge statue was seen by Russian thinkers and writers as a metaphor for Russia itself and the direction in which Peter and his successors were taking the country and its people. Alexander Nikolaevich Radishchev (1749–1802) was one of the intellectuals who remarked on it. Radishchev received the ire of Catherine the Great and ten years in Siberian exile for his 1790 work *Journey from Petersburg*, which criticized serfdom and the Russian autocracy. Radishchev told a friend:

> The steepness of the hill [the stone base] symbolizes the obstacles lying in Peter's way.... The snake represents perfidy and malice which sought to punish Peter with death for the introduction of the new ways. His clothes of ancient cut, the bearskin, and the simplicity of the horse's harness and of the rider's attire point to the simple and coarse manners and the ignorance which Peter found in the populace and which he wanted to reform.... His spirited countenance shows the inner conviction of someone who has fulfilled his goals, while the extended arm is protective and betrays a man of strength, one who has overcome all the obstacles along his way and who is now offering refuge to those who would call themselves his children. (Cited in Schenker 295)

Pushkin's poem is the origin of the "myth of Petersburg"—an abiding literary identity for the city found in the vibrating tension between the dualities of glittering imperial order and dark chaotic dissolution, the quotidian and the fantastic, the real and the unreal. In this work Pushkin addresses some of the greatest issues in Russian history: the importance of Peter himself and his Westernizing reforms, the relationship between the individual and the state, and the heroic drive to create, despite the havoc wreaked upon lives fated to be either the means or the ends of those creations.

PUSHKIN AND ADAM MICKIEWICZ

Pushkin's poem was actually not the first inspired by the statue. In 1832, the year before Pushkin wrote *The Bronze Horseman*, Polish romantic poet Adam Mickiewicz (1798–1855) published the poem *The Monument of Peter the Great*. Like Pushkin, Mickiewicz is also held to be the greatest poet of his nation. At the time both poems were written, eastern Poland was ruled by the Russian tsar—Catherine colluded with Prussia and Austria in dividing up between them Poland, one of Europe's oldest states. Mickiewich had been exiled to Russia in 1824 from Russian-held Poland. In the years until his departure from Russia to Western Europe in 1829 he became well known in the brilliant and fashionable social and intellectual circles of Moscow and St. Petersburg, where he became friends with Pushkin.

In his poem, Mickiewicz describes a meeting between himself ("that pilgrim from a western land") and "the famous Russian bard"—Pushkin, who speaks most of poem's words. Dismayed at Russia's imperial ambitions and its authoritarian government, Mickiewicz has Pushkin express the hope that Western European cultural and political influences will lead Russia to change course:

> His charger's reins Tsar Peter has released;
> He has been flying down the road, perchance,
> And here the precipice checks his advance.

With hoofs aloft now stands the maddened beast,
Champing its bit unchecked, with slackened rein:
You guess that it will fall and be destroyed.
Thus it has galloped long, with tossing mane,
Like a cascade, leaping into the void,
That, fettered by the frost, hangs dizzily.
But soon will shine the sun of liberty,
And from the west a wind will warm this land.—
Will the cascade of tyranny then stand?
(Mickiewicz 350)

On the face of it, Pushkin's poem is a polemic with that of his Polish friend. In several poems published after Mickiewicz left Russia, Pushkin condemned the 1830 Polish uprising and praised Russia's action to put it down. Pushkin thus may have felt Mickiewicz's poem was actually a criticism of Pushkin himself. Pushkin was no supporter of Russian autocracy, though he did love his home city, and his poem works less as a defense of Peter than of Petersburg itself. Ultimately, Pushkin is engaged in much more than an agon with Mickiewicz. *The Bronze Horseman* is richer in style than *The Monument of Peter the Great*, more complex in its formal aspects, and aesthetically more satisfying. Its setting is the massive Petersburg flood of 1824 that cast much of the city under water. It describes the fate of an insignificant clerk, Evgeny, who one night has a fateful encounter with the statue. In the poem's long introduction, a paean to the city, the strong, noble Peter contemplates with barely-contained energy the building of a city on a spot where only a poor fishermen's village stood:

On a shore washed by desolate waves, *he* stood,
Full of high thoughts, and gazed into the distance
(Pushkin 247).

The narrator sings the praises of the city, the Neva and its banks—here awash with light during the summer's white nights:

> I love you, Peter's creation, I love your stern
> Harmonious look, the Neva's majestic flow,
> Her granite banks, the iron tracery
> Of your railings, the transparent twilight and
> The moonless glitter of your pensive nights
>
> ...
>
> Flaunt your beauty, Peter's
> City, and stand unshakable like Russia,
> So that even the conquered elements may make
> Their peace with you ... (Pushkin 248–249)

At the height of the storm during which the poem's primary action takes place, Evgeny finds himself astride one of several carved lions on a high porch of a palace in the square containing the statue. After the worst of the deluge is past, Evgeny discovers that the rushing waters and whipping wind have swept away the shack where his love, and hoped-for wife, lived. With hopes for happiness dashed and mind shaken, Evgeny takes to wandering the city as a vagabond. One gloomy, wet fall night he wakens on the Neva embankment, and with a start he sees he has wandered onto the square over which the visage of the dread emperor is eternally cast:

> ... Terribly his thoughts
> Grew clear in him. He recognized the place
> Where the flood played, where greedy waves had pressed,
> Rioting round him angrily, and the lions,
> And the square, and him who motionlessly
> Held aloft his bronze head in the darkness,
> Him by whose fateful will the city had
> Been founded on the sea ... How terrible
> He was in the surrounding murk! What thought

Was on his brow, what strength was hidden in him!
And in that steed what fire! Where do you gallop,
Proud steed, and where will you plant your hoofs?
O mighty master of fate! was it not thus,
Towering on the precipice's brink,
You reared up Russia with your iron curb? (Pushkin 256)

His wits now entirely gone, Evgeny runs, convinced the
dread tsar is thundering after him:

... Across the empty square
He runs, and hears behind him—like the rumble
Of thunder—the clash and clangor of hoofs
Heavily galloping over the shaking square.
And lit by the pale moonlight, stretching out
His hand aloft, the Bronze Horseman rushes
After him on his ponderously galloping mount;
And all night long, wherever the madman ran,
The Bronze Horseman followed with a ringing clatter.
(Pushkin 257)

Evgeny continues to be pursued by the equestrian Peter until
finally his corpse is found on the spot where his fiancée's hut
once stood.

Pushkin's poetic meditation on the statute is seen as a
metaphor for the identity and fate of Russia, the hubris and
greatness of its most compelling ruler, and the place of the individual facing the vast energy and power through which nations
and great cities are created. Emperor Nicholas I, Catherine's
grandson, himself read Pushkin's poem in manuscript. Con-
cerned that Pushkin was voicing opposition to Peter, and thus
criticism of the Russian autocracy as an institution and of
Nicholas himself, the emperor forbade publication. Shortly
after Pushkin's death in a duel in 1837, the work was finally
published.

The synergy of monument and poem is remarkable, and the

statue is known today by the name of the poem that commemorates it. Pushkin's poem and Falconet's statue echo throughout Russian literature of the 19th and 20th centuries.

The Literary Cafe

On the corner of Nevsky Prospect and the Moika Canal stands the illustrious Literary Cafe. It is here, past simple archways into an elegant dining room, that Russia's greatest poet Alexander Pushkin had a bite to eat before walking out into the snowy St. Petersburg night to die at the hands of an enemy in a duel. The year was 1837.

The Literary Cafe had opened as a confectioners only two years before. Other Russian literary figures, such as Dostoevksy and Alexander Chernyshevsky, enjoyed the posh atmosphere of the café as well. Vaulted ceilings, parquet floors, bronze candelabras, gleaming sconces, crisp linens were all a part of St. Petersburg's most elaborate literary setting.

Even in the waning days of the Soviet empire, the Literary Cafe was an oasis in a desert of stagnation. While shops were bare and whatever restaurant food was available was of questionable quality, the Literary Cafe served up delicate canapés with small dabs of caviar, the usual tomato and cucumber salad, but with an elegant flair, tender blini, and small chunks of succulent sturgeon. It wouldn't have earned a single Michelin star, but the atmosphere was always elegant, subdued, and superbly humane in a growingly inhumane society. Poets, writers, theater actors, and tourists frequented this historical venue.

Today, with a proliferation of new and modern cafés, clubs, and restaurants around the city, the Literary Cafe maintains a lower profile, with an upstairs dining room featuring chamber music in the evenings. The many vaulted rooms have been closed off by a wall. That space now houses a private company.

Russia's greatest poet of the early 20th century, the symbolist Alexander Blok, referring to both works of art, declared, "*The Bronze Horseman*—we are all in the vibrations of its bronze.*"

ANDREI BELY

In the early 20th century, the Russian symbolist writer Andrei Bely felt the monument's vibrations strongly, conveying them in his masterwork, *Petersburg* (1913–1914, revised in 1922). Bely's novel is one of the great modernist novels along with those of Joyce, Kakfa, and Proust. As one of the novel's characters, Alexander Ivanovich, hurries home to escape the chaos on the streets of revolutionary Petrograd, he, like Pushkin's Evgeny, has an encounter with Peter. The passage, which was clearly for Bely one of the most important in the book, is worth quoting at length. Echoing Pushkin's lines, Bely adopts a prophetic voice in addressing the fate of Russia. Central to the images of the passage is the notion, common not only in Bely's time but today as well, that through his Westernizing reforms Peter wrested Russia from its roots in the common Russian people (the *narod*), turning the country onto unnatural paths of development.

> Beyond the bridge, against the background of St. Isaac's, a crag rose out of the murk. Extending a heavy patinated hand, the enigmatic Horseman loomed; the horse flung out two hooves above the shaggy fur hat of a Palace grenadier; and the grenadier's shaggy fur hat swayed beneath the hooves.
>
> A shadow concealed the enormous face of the Horseman. A palm cut into the moonlit air.
>
> From that fecund time when the metallic Horseman had galloped hither, when he had flung his steed upon the Finnish granite, Russia was divided in two. Divided in two as well were the destinies of the fatherland. Suffering and weeping, Russia was divided in two, until the final hour.
>
> Russia, you are the steed! Your two front hooves have

leaped far off into the darkness, into the void, while your two rear hooves are firmly implanted in the granite soil.

Do you want to separate yourself from the rock that holds you, as some of your mad sons have separated themselves from the soil? Do you too want to separate yourself from the rock that holds you, and hang, bridleless, suspended in air, and then plunge down into the chaos of waters? Or, could it be that you want to hurtle through the air, cleaving the mists, to disappear in the clouds along with your sons? Or having reared up, have you, oh Russia, fallen deep into thought for long years in the face of the awesome fate that has cast you here, amidst this gloomy north, where even the sunset itself lasts many hours, where time itself in turn pitches now into frosty night, now into diurnal radiance? Or will you, taking fright at the leap, again set down your hooves and, snorting, now out of control, carry off the great Horseman, out of these illusory lands into the depths of plain-flat spaces?

May this not come to pass!

Once it has soared up on its hind legs, measuring the air with its eyes, the bronze steed will not set down its hooves. There will be a leap across history. Great shall be the turmoil. The earth shall be cleft. The very mountains shall be thrown down by the cataclysmic earthquake, and because of that earthquake our native plains will everywhere come forth humped....

As for Petersburg, it will sink. (Bely 64–65)

DECEMBRISTS SQUARE

The view that Petersburg is an unnatural city, foreign to those Russians who remained true to traditional Russian cultural mores, was widespread throughout the 19th and early 20th century. In the Soviet period this opinion was in some ways reversed, as well shall later see in this book.

The magnificent square over which Peter looks, forever poised on his rearing steed, has its own dramatic history. Like the city itself, it has been known by several names. Today it is called both by its Soviet-era name, Decembrists Square, and by its primary tsarist-era name, Senate Square, received by virtue of the large building of the Imperial Senate located on one side of the square. On December 14, 1825, several hundred elite guardsmen, their heads full of dreams of liberalism and the possibility of political reform in Russia, the likes of which they had seen in Europe while on campaign against Napoleon, attempted an ill-fated coup on Senate Square. The timing of their action was forced on them by outside events: Alexander I unexpectedly died in November and his brother Nicholas, the next in the line of succession, quickly arranged for a public ceremony for December 14 on Senate Square, at which he would be declared emperor and accept the declaration of loyalty from his troops. When several thousand soldiers followed their noble officers into rebellion, the scene on the square was set for a dramatic confrontation. After several hours, the exasperated Nicholas ordered cannon be fired at the rebels, who scattered at "whiff of grapeshot," in the description of a loyalist. In the melee that followed on the square and the streets leading away from it, some 1,200 were killed, mainly rebels, but also some bystanders. Five of the instigators were later executed, 31 were exiled to Siberia for life, and 85 more were given shorter sentences of exile. In many cases, the condemned were accompanied on the long road to Siberia by their wives and families.

These "Decembrists" as they came to be called, were the immediate predecessors of that particularly Russian phenomenon of the *intelligentsia*, an intellectual elite opposed to autocratic rule. As a Romantic image, their actions and fate echo resoundingly through Russian culture of the 19th century. Alexander Pushkin had been educated in the spirit of liberal thought common among many Russian noblemen of the early nineteenth century, and a voice critical of autocracy and the institutions supporting it, particularly serfdom, was often strong in his verse. Especially well known were these final lines of his *Ode to Liberty* (1817), which was inspired by a similarly named poem by Radishchev:

> And now know this, O Tsars:
> Neither punishments nor rewards
> Nor prison bars nor altars
> Will protect you any more.
> Be the first to bow your heads
> To the trustworthy force of the Law,
> And then the eternal defender of your throne
> Will be the peace and liberty of the people.

Pushkin's poems with similar political content were well known throughout Petersburg society. Decembrist Ivan Yakushkin later recalled: "Once could scarcely find a literate ensign in the army who did not know them by heart." Pushkin himself was not a member of the Decembrists' circle, and on the day of the revolt was at his family's estate two hundred miles from Petersburg, having been exiled from the capital for his politically sensitive verse. Another poet, Kondraty Ryleev, was a leader among the Decembrists, and one of the five to be executed. Pushkin reportedly later told Nicholas that had he been in Petersburg that fateful day in December 1825, he would have joined the rebels. Certainly the poet was deeply influenced by the revolt, and the sense of Senate Square as a place of darkness, fraught with danger, is clearly evident in the masterpiece he wrote eight years later.

ALEXANDER HERZEN

On this square the nineteenth-century Russian thinker, dissident, and writer Alexander Herzen (1812–1870) began his acquaintance with the city as a young man. A native Muscovite, Herzen was sent by his father in 1839 to conduct affairs for him in the Russian capital. As he recounts his visit to the square in his memoir, *My Past and Thoughts*, considered to be both a literary and historical classic, Herzen's mind is filled with thoughts of the bloody scene of December 1825 and the poetry of his friend Nikolai Ogarev:

> When I reached Petersburg at nine o'clock in the evening, I took an *izvozchik* [a hired cab] and drove to St Isaac's Square. I wanted that to be the place with which I was to begin my acquaintance with Petersburg. Everything was covered with deep snow, only Peter I on his horse, gloomy and menacing, stood out sharply against the grey background in the darkness of the night.

> And looming black through mists of night
> With stately poise and haughty mein,
> Pointing afar with outstretched hand,
> A warrior on a horse is seen,
> A mighty figure, bold and free.
> The steed is reined. It rears aloft
> And paws the air imperiously,
> So that its lord might further see.
> Ogarev.

Herzen continues his meditation:

> Why was it that the conflict of the 14th of December took place on that square? Why was it from that pedestal that the first cry of Russian freedom rang out? Why did the square of soldiers press close round Peter I? Was it his reward ... or his punishment? The 14th of December, 1825, was the sequel of the work interrupted on the 21st of January, 1725. Nicholas's guns were turned upon the insurrection and upon the statue alike; it is a pity that the grapeshot did not shoot down the bronze Peter.... (Herzen 426–427)

Herzen was correct in associating this part of the city with the powerful tsarist state itself, of which he became an implacable foe, issuing trenchant criticism from his self-imposed London exile in the 1850s and 1860s in his newspaper "The Bell," (*Kolokol*), issues of which were smuggled into Russia and then read widely. The northwest side of Decembrists Square is fronted by a building whose roots lay at the center of Peter's plan for his northern capital on the Baltic Sea: the Admiralty (*Admiralteistvo*). The over 400-yard-long building extends northeast along the embankment of the Neva, reaching nearly to the Palace Square. Here in 1711 Peter built the headquarters for his navy, and though reconstructed and expanded in the early 19th century, the Admiralty continued in this function until 1917. The most notable feature of the building, a fine example of the Russian Empire style, is perhaps its graceful gilded spire; as the Admiralty is the focal point of three of St. Petersburg's major streets—Nevsky Prospect, Gorokhova Street,

The Neva

Petersburg sits on the delta of the Neva River, which flows from nearby Lake Ladoga into the Gulf of Finland, the arm of the Baltic Sea that extends eastward between Finland and Estonia, reaching Russia at its easternmost tip. The land surrounding the mouth of the Neva is low and marshy (*neva* is a Finnic word meaning "swamp" or "bog") and is subject to periodic flooding. Thus it seems Petersburg is indeed a city molded by man from the ocean.

The Neva is easily the largest waterway within the cluster of delta islands that make up the city. Ranging in breadth from 1,300 to 2,600 feet, it provides Petersburg some of its most impressive vistas. Along the granite embankments of the Neva are arrayed some of the city's most notable landmarks, including the Winter Palace, the Summer Gardens, the Admiralty, the Peter and Paul Fortress, and the Menshikov Palace. The Neva serves as a major traffic artery. It reaches nearly 80 feet in depth, making it navigable by large and small vessels and Voznesensky Prospect—this spire is clearly visible from much of the central parts of the city. The large grounds of the Admiralty are a favorite park among Petersburg's residents, and couples love to stroll here, surrounded by trees and statues and busts of leading figures from Russia's past, primarily cultural greats, notably the composer Glinka and the writers Gogol and Lermontov. The Admirality is the subject of a poem by the great Osip Mandelshtam, discussed in Chapter 6.

AROUND THE BRONZE HORSEMAN

The area around the Bronze Horseman is noted for a number of other buildings that radiate the power and grandeur of the Russian state in the nineteenth century. St. Isaac's Cathedral is certainly one of these. Named for a Byzantine monk whose

alike. Except during winter months when the river is frozen, large cargo ships ply its waters at night; the bridges which span it are raised to allow them passage.

The Neva and its major tributaries divide the city into its major districts. Vasilievsky Island (*Vasilevsky ostrov*) is the large, triangular wedge of land that juts westward into the Gulf of Finland. On the right bank of the Neva to the northeast is the Vyborg Side (*Vyborgskaya storona*), named after a city 75 miles northwest of Petersburg. On the northern bank of the Neva, between Vasilievsky Island and the Vyborg Side, lies a group of islands that together comprise the Petrograd Side (*Petrogradskaya storona*). The southernmost of these is the small Zayachy Island; in 1703 on this strategically advantageous spot Peter the Great erected a fortress, the birthplace of his new city. The following year he built the original Admiralty on the Neva embankment across from Vasilievsky Island, and here, on the southern bank of the Neva, the grand imperial center of Petersburg was built.

name day according to the Orthodox calendar was the day on which Peter the Great was born (May 30), this vast neo-classical structure, with its gold dome soaring 110 yards into the air, dominates the city's skyline. The cathedral is generally associated with reign of the authoritarian Nicholas I, though construction was actually begun before his reign and was completed only after his death in 1855. On the cathedral's square, some 400 yards from the Bronze Horseman, an uninspired statue of a mounted Nicholas stands guard. This equestrian emperor, however, rides unheralded by Russia's writers, whom he so vigorously sought to repress.

The magnificent neo-classical building on the square's southwest side was built between 1829 and 1834 by Italian architect Italo Rossi, who also designed the General Staff building across from the Hermitage on Palace Square, and housed the Russian Senate and Holy Synod. Founded by Peter the Great in 1711 as a body for civil administration, it soon became a judicial body only. The Holy Synod was also established by Peter, in 1721, to administer the affairs of the Orthodox Church in Russia. These buildings today house the Russian State Historical Archive and its vast collection of documents, which primarily date from the tsarist period, though use of them will soon pass to the Russian Presidential Administration.

Directly opposite St. Isaac's Cathedral to the east is the Lobanov-Rostovsky House, a mansion built in 1817–1820. It is noted for the two stone lions before the building's columned portico, challenging all who draw near. In *The Bronze Horseman*, Pushkin's hero Evgeny finds himself here after a night of aimless wandering, still unable to escape Peter:

> He found himself at the foot of the pillars of
> The great house. Over the porch the lions stood
> On guard, like living creatures, with their paws
> Upraised; and eminently dark and high
> Above the railed-in rock, with arm outstretched,

The Image, mounted on his horse of bronze.
(Pushkin 256)

On the east side of St. Isaac's Square is the Astoria Hotel, the most famous hotel in all of St. Petersburg. Completed in the early twentieth century, some of Petersburg's most illustrious guests have stayed here, including the great Russian writers Maxim Gorky and Mikhail Bulgakov, in addition to other leading Russian artists. The English novelist H.G. Wells and the American writer and political radical John Reed also were guests, as were many other important political figures. In an annex of the Astoria that once was a separate hotel, the Russian poet Sergei Yesenin (1895–1925), bard of Russian rural life and one-time husband of American dancer Isadora Duncan, committed suicide. He left a poem written in his own blood: "In this life it is not new to die, / But neither is it new to be alive."

CHAPTER FOUR

Nevsky Prospect
and the Petersburg
of Nikolai Gogol

The literary image of Petersburg and its myth as a place of both dream and reality has their genesis in the work of Pushkin. Russian literary scholar N.P. Antsiferov wrote in his influential study *The Spirit of Petersburg* (Petersburg 1922) that Pushkin was "in the same measure the creator of the image of Petersburg as Peter the Great was the builder of the city itself" (40). Pushkin's contemporary, Nikolai Vasilevich Gogol (1809–1852) further elaborated the myth of the city, and in doing so introduced both to Russian and world literature some remarkable narrative techniques, particularly in his use of irrationality and even mental illness as lenses through which his tales are told. While Pushkin is indeed the foundational writer for the modern Russian literary language, his influence is minimal beyond the Russian literary world. The literary progeny of Gogol, however, are significant both within Russia and without, and like the seed of a Biblical patriarch, have only grown with time. Dostoevsky is surely the most prominent of Gogol's Russian descendants in the nineteenth century; in the twentieth century these include a host of Soviet Russia's best writers: Andrei Bely, Mikhail Bulgakov, Andrei Platonov, and others. Gogol's fantastic and grotesque view of the world and mankind has left a wide mark on the literatures of many languages, and the works of many important 20h century writers would be impossible were it not for his precedent. Kafka stands out as the most prominent, though the entire schools of absurdism and magical realism are in Gogol's debt.

St. Petersburg and its denizens occupy a place of central concern in Gogol's work. Born into a poor gentry family not far from Poltava, in the Ukraine, Gogol came to Petersburg at age nineteen in 1828 seeking a brilliant career, though he seemed not quite sure at first what that career would be. Two volumes of stories enlivened with the culture and language of his native Ukraine, published in 1831 and 1832, established Gogol as a successful writer. But it is his cycle of Petersburg stories, appearing between 1835 and 1842, that made clear Gogol's greatness. In these tales, several of which number among the greatest short stories written in any language, Gogol expands upon the Pushkinian theme of mythic and fantastical Petersburg. But while Pushkin's *Bronze Horseman* primarily probes the tensions the individual experiences with society and the state, Gogol's Petersburg stories plumb deeper psychologically, particularly in their treatment of the often trivial, but also disturbing conflict between human expectation and the fabric of reality, as well as in their examination of environment and locale upon the development of human irrationality. Gogol scholar Donald Fanger writes that Gogol "was a mythographer of the city, evoking it through a highly personal vision, the chief element of which—as Andrey Bely pointed out—is terror and the chief theme, kinlessness and alienation.... Gogol is giving us a city of the mind, deprived of grace, and superimposing it on the map and mores of Petersburg...." (Fanger 120)

NEVSKY PROSPECT

Gogol's story "Nevsky Prospect" (sometimes translated as "Nevsky Avenue") begins and ends with descriptions of life on this central boulevard in Petersburg, and in it the writer lays out his artistic view of the city, providing bookends describing the world inhabited by the characters of the story. The story's opening lines seem flattering, and they are often quoted by tourist guides to the city. But recommending this story to visitors to the city might be reckless; not only is the opening passage ironic, but it abounds in the weird sort of details that mark the Gogolian phantasmagoria:

> There is nothing better than Nevsky Prospect, at least not in Petersburg; for there it is everything. What does this street— the beauty of our capital—not shine with! I know that not one of its pale and clerical inhabitants would trade Nevsky Prospect for anything in the world. Not only the one who is twenty-five years old, has an excellent mustache and a frock coat of an amazing cut, but even the one who has white hair sprouting on his chin and a head as smooth as a silver dish, he, too, is enchanted with Nevsky Prospect. And the ladies! Oh, the ladies find Nevsky Prospect still more pleasing. And who does not find it pleasing? (Gogol 245)

Nevsky Prospect is the most famous street in Petersburg, a sort of Champs Elysée for this city, which for over two hundred years was the capital of the Russian empire. The street is nearly three miles long, extending straight as an arrow for one and a quarter miles from the Admiralty to the Square of the Uprising (*ploshchad' Vosstaniia*), called Znamensky Square in the tsarist period. The boulevard then turns a few degrees to the south, at which point its grandeur trails off for the rest of its length, though the far southeastern terminus is the important Alexander Nevsky Monastery, which is also located near the banks of the Neva River as it bends southward. Here many cultural luminaries of the nineteenth century are buried, including Dostoevsky, the painters Kustodiev and Serov, and most of the country's leading composers of the pre-Soviet era, including Glinka, Rimsky-Korsakov, Musorgsky, Borodin, and Tchaikovsky.

Nevsky Prospect is named after the 13th-century Russian prince Alexander Nevsky, who in 1240 defeated a Swedish force advancing up the Neva River, thereby earning his nickname, which means "of the Neva." Two years later he and his forces vanquished an army of Teutonic Knights on an ice-covered Lake Peipus, which straddles the Russian-Estonian border to the southwest from where nearly half a millennium later Petersburg would rise. (Director Sergei Eisenstein's immortalized this battle in his 1938 film "Alexander Nevsky"; Sergei Prokoviev's cantata of the same name accompanied the film.)

Originally called "Great Perspective Road," the street was renamed in 1738 to "Neva Perspective Road," and then two decades later to Nevsky Prospect. Following the Bolshevik Revolution, the new political leadership officially renamed the street "25 October Avenue," after the date in the prevailing Julian calendar on which the Bolsheviks seized power in this city, then called "Petrograd." This new name never took hold, however, and its name was again officially changed to Nevsky Prospect in 1944.

Peter the Great intended his new capital to be a second Amsterdam, with long, straight thoroughfares intersecting rings of canals. And indeed, a comparison of the maps of the central sections of each city bears out a remarkable similarity, with the Neva River a rough (and much larger) parallel to the Amstel. The construction of Nevsky Prospect was a prime example of Peter the Great's application of Enlightenment ideals in city planning; clean, straight lines instead of the hodgepodge of curved roads and narrow alleyways in cities such as Moscow. The earliest section of Nevsky Prospect to be laid out was its northwest end, in 1715; the street served as a new highway leading out of Petersburg towards Novgorod and Moscow. Nevsky quickly became one of the city's most noteworthy sights. Diarist Friedrich Wilhelm von Bergholtz, a German who lived much of his life in Russia, recorded in the early 1720s his impressions of the "long, wide avenue paved in stone":

Notwithstanding that the three or four rows of trees on either side of it are still not large, it is extraordinarily beautiful by reason of its enormous extent and state of cleanliness ... It makes a more wonderful sight than any I have ever beheld anywhere." (Cracraft 149)

AROUND NEVSKY

The glory of Nevsky Prospect is contained in its "Parade section," the mile-long stretch from the Admiralty, whose spire rises at the very head of the street and is visible down its length, to the Fontanka River (actually a canal), which intersects it at right angles. Most impressive are the several palaces in the neoclassical and rococo styles built here in the mid-18th century. As Gogol was writing his Petersburg stories, the greatest of these palaces were the Anichkov Palace, near the Fontanka, and the Stroganov Palace, on the banks of the River Moika (also a canal), which Nevsky crosses near the head of the street. Built in the 1740s by the empress Elizabeth for her lover, Aleksei Razumovsky, and later in the century given by Catherine the Great to her lover, Grigory Potemkin, the neoclassical Anichkov Palace was home to many young princes, including the son of Nicholas I, the future Alexander III, who continued to live here even after assuming the throne in 1881. Today the palace houses a children's organization. The baroque Stroganov Palace was built in 1752–54 by Rastrelli, the architect of the Winter Palace, for the fantastically wealthy fur-trading Stroganov family; it now houses part of the collection of the Russian Museum. Just over the Anichkov Bridge with its equestrian statues is perhaps the most striking palace on Nevsky Prospect, the neo-baroque Belosersky-Belozersky palace, whose oxide red exterior causes the building to glow at sunset. Inspired by the Stroganov palace, the Belosersky-Belozersky Palace was built between 1846 and 1848, over a decade after Gogol's Petersburg tales were published.

As readers of Gogol know, Nevsky Prospect was far from

being the bailiwick solely of Petersburg's wealthy nobles. In the eighteenth century the city's merchant class had its center in this section of the city, and fronting the street is the merchant's hall, *Gostinyi dvor*, completed in the 1780s, it replacing an earlier structure. The classical facades of this sprawling, two-story building total some 1,000 yards in circumference. The nearby Kazan Cathedral, built in the early nineteenth century, resembles a scaled-down, but nonetheless impressive version of St. Peter's in the Vatican City. Both of these landmarks, publicly accessible today as in tsarist times, are scenes of action in Gogol's Petersburg story "The Nose." Throughout its existence, this section of Nevsky Prospect has been the place individuals of nearly all social stations stroll about—both to see those with whom they share this city and to be seen by others in turn.

A TYPICAL DAY ON GOGOL'S NEVSKY

In the era Gogol was writing, what people could be found walking along the trottoirs of Nevsky Prospect? In his study *Sunlight at Midnight: St. Petersburg and the Rise of Modern Russia*, prolific historian of Russia the late W. Bruce Lincoln colorfully evokes of the passage of a day along the street as Gogol would have seen it in the 1830s and 1840s. In the mornings the street was filled with simple working people, especially peasants working on the numerous building sites in Petersburg, many of which involved the labor of thousands; indeed, it was largely due to their presence that out of the some half million residents of Petersburg in the 1840s, seven out of ten were men and more than two fifths were of the peasant estate.[1] Servants, bakers, waiters, and other lower-level workers also hurried to their places of employment. Draymen and hackney drivers took their places along the street, waiting for their fares, most of which would come along in the later morning as "proper society" in the city began to move about and as bureaucrats began to make their way to their offices. Later in the morning, shopkeepers and tradesmen opened their establishments for customers, and artisans hurried to their work benches. Towards noon, children of Petersburg's wealthy class emerged, accompanied by their private tutors and governesses, many of whom were foreigners, retained to help their charges learn proper French or English. Civil servants could most frequently be seen on Nevsky in the afternoon. With the waning of the light of day (which happened early in the afternoon in the dark winters of Petersburg), the street took on an entirely new look under the light of street lamps, which only recently had arrived in the city. Now a unpredictable mélange of people could be seen on the street. It was Nevsky lit by street lamps that most fascinated Gogol.

The unending variety of life in the city transfixed Gogol, who indeed remained a country boy wide-eyed in wonder at life in the big city. In a letter home to his mother shortly after arriving in Petersburg, Gogol described the diversity held within the walls of the building in a less prestigous section of the city in which he rented an upper-story room (the place in a building where the indigent often lived):

> The house in which I live contains two tailors, one *marchand de mode*, a shoemaker, a hosiery manufacturer, a repairer of broken dishes, a plasterer, and a house painter, a pastry shop, a notions shop, a cold storage for winter clothing, a tobacco shop, and finally, a midwife for the privileged. Naturally, this building has to be plastered all over with gold signs. I live on the fourth floor (Volkov, *St. Petersburg* 26).

Gogol remained interested primarily in the lower class of Petersburg; the life of the powerful—the aristocracy, small in number (only about 50,000 at mid-century), and the highest level of civil servants—did not capture his imagination. Gogol failed at a number of professions after arriving in the city—actor, lower-level bureaucrat, teacher. His sympathies lay with these folk, those who barely made ends meet, with those like the anti-hero of his story, "The Overcoat," an obscure clerk for whom a well-made coat was an expensive luxury.

GOGOL AND THE NIKOLAEAN ERA

The Pushkinian duality of St. Petersburg that informs "The Bronze Horseman" is further developed in Gogol's story "Nevsky Prospect," one of the first in the Petersburg cycle to be published, and an excellent introduction to life in the city in the Nikolaean era. The story's heroes, Piskarev, an artist, and Pirogov, an army lieutenant, espy two attractive young women whom they then pursue. The fates of the two friends then wildly diverge, one turning tragic, the other broadly comedic. The dark-haired beauty coveted by Piskarev turns out to be a prostitute, and in despair at the fate of his hoped-for beloved, the young man commits suicide. The blond prey of Pirogov turns out to be the wife of a local German artisan. When this otherwise upstanding and sober-minded artisan together with two friends arrives home drunk one day to find Pirogov dancing with his wife, the three promptly administer the officer a sound and humiliating beating. Of Pirogov's fate the reader is told only that upon returning home he entertained the ludicrous intention of complaining to the army General Staff in hope it would defend his honor.

The narrator of "Nevsky Prospect" then comments on the stories he has just related:

"Marvelous is the working of our world," I thought as I walked down Nevsky Prospect two days ago, calling to mind these two events. "How strangely, how inconceivably our fate plays with us! Do we ever get what we desire? Do we ever achieve that for which our powers seem purposely to prepare us? Everything happens in a contrary way. To this one fate gave wonderful horses, and he drives around indifferently without ever noticing their beauty—while another, whose heart burns with the horse passion, goes on foot and contents himself with merely clicking his tongue as a trotter is led past him. This one has an excellent cook, but unfortunately so small a mouth that it cannot let pass more than a couple of tidbits; another has a mouth as big as the archway of general headquarters, but, alas! has to be satisified with some German dinner of potatoes. How strangely our fate plays with us!" (Gogol 277)

The contingency of human experience integral to the Gogolian grammar of story-telling has a very contemporary feel to it and goes a long way in explaining the writer's enduring power. Also striking is Gogol's depiction of the seemingly random nature of the fabric of life. In the introduction to the wonderful new translation of Gogol's collected stories by Richard Pevear and Larissa Volokhonsky, Pevear points out that Gogol's status as an outsider in Petersburg—he never was fully accepted into the social circles of the capital, and the world of Petersburg officialdom was also closed to him—actually helped him not only to further his art, but also to become a recognizably modern writer:

[I]ndeed, Gogol's art, despite its romantic ghosts and folkloric trappings, is strikingly modern in two ways: first, his works are free verbal creations, based on their own premises rather than on the conventions of nineteenth-century fiction; and second, they are highly theatrical in presentation, concentrated on figures and gestures, constructed in a way that, while admitting any amount of digression, precludes the social and psychological analysis of classical realism. His images remain ambiguous and uninterpreted, which is what makes them loom so large before us. (Gogol ix)

Gogol posits that the surest wager is not to trust the accepted and seeming obvious networks of relationships between objects, human beings, and places that are offered up to us by daily life:

But strangest of all are the events that take place on Nevsky Prospect. Oh, do not believe this Nevsky Prospect! I always wrap myself tighter in my cloak and try not to look at the objects I meet at all. Everything is deception, everything is a dream, everything is not what it seems to be! (Gogol 277)

In the brilliant final paragraph of the story that begins with the lines just cited, Gogol describes more of the phantoms of reality that one can see by the street lamps of Nevsky Prospect and then counsels the reader to dismiss them:

> Further away, for God's sake, further away from the street lamp! pass it by more quickly, as quickly as possible. You'll be lucky to get away with it pouring its stinking oil on your foppish frock coat. But, along with the street lamp, everything breathes deceit. It lies all the time, this Nevsky Prospect, but most of all at the time when night heaves its dense mass upon it and sets off the white and pale yellow walls of the houses, when the whole city turns into a rumbling and brilliance, myriads of carriages tumble from the bridges, postillions shout and bounce on their horses, and the devil himself lights the lamps only so as to show everything not as it really looks. (Gogol 278)

Urban theorist Marshall Berman has written incisively on the illusive nature of Gogol's Nevsky Prospect and of the nature of human experience there:

> There are several paradoxes about Nevsky's sociability. On the one hand, it brings people face to face with each other; on the other hand, it propels people past each other with such speed and force that it's hard for anyone to look at anyone closely—before you can focus clearly, the apparition is gone. Hence much of the vision that the Nevsky affords is a vision not so much of the people presenting themselves as of fragmented forms and features flashing by. (Berman 196)

In a major critical work on Gogol published in 1944, Vladimir Nabokov wrote that Gogol saw Petersburg as "a reflection in a blurred mirror, an eerie medley of objects put to the wrong use, things going backwards the faster they moved

Train Travel

St. Petersburg and Moscow are inextricably linked by the emperors of Russia. Trading off as capitals, as well as Russia's first and second cities—though Moscow by far outraced St. Petersburg in terms of population long ago—both metropoli are the best representations of Russia past and present. As for tourists, most visitors to Russia wouldn't dream of visiting one city without the other. And rightly so ... both cities, collectively, encompass the history of the Russian and Soviet Empires. And the best way to travel between the two is by train.

During Soviet times, residents of "Pieter"(the nickname that remained even when the city was called Leningrad), regularly trekked to Moscow for shopping. Invariably the goods were more plentiful and of better quality than outside the capital. Muscovites who yearned to get away from the gray monotony of their inner city visited Leningrad to witness the White Nights in the summer. Even when the Soviet system didn't work, the trains did—always on time, and always with a steaming "stakanchik" of tea waiting for weary travelers.

St. Petersburg has five train stations, with the Moscow Station being one of the busiest. After 1991 a great bust of Lenin in the center of the station was replaced by Peter the Great—to greet visitors disembarking from the Red Arrow (Krasnaya Strela) overnight train from Moscow. Passengers are given sheets and blankets, and can request "soft" class with only two berths, second class with four, or "platskartny"—a full wagon with wooden benches for a number of people. The Red Arrow shuttles between the two cities, departing at 11:55 P.M. and arriving just after eight in the morning. In Moscow, it arrives at the Leningrad Station, greeted by a bust of—who else—but Lenin. A day train, the Aurora, travels between the cities in half the time.

forward, pale gray nights instead of ordinary black ones, and black days." (Nabokov 12)

The German cultural historian Karl Schlögel argues that the first half of the 19th century was the "golden era" of cultural life on Nevsky Prospect. The spirit of the street had changed from what it was in the 18th century; the center of life on Nevsky had shifted from the opulent palaces to more mundane places, particularly the apartments, cafés and bookstores frequented by writers and artists. A favorite meeting place of the literary intelligentsia was the Wolf and Beranger confectionary shop, located on Nevsky near the intersection with the Moika River (Nevsky Prospect No. 15). Pushkin met here with his second, two days before his death in the duel with d'Anthes, after which Lermontov read his poem "Death of the Poet." A building a bit further down the street (Nevsky Prospect No. 30) housed a famous bookstore owned by A.F. Smirdin. Regular customers included Pushkin, the fabulist I.A. Krylov (1769–1844), and the poet V.A. Zhukovsky (1783–1852).

Further down the street, on the corner of Nevsky and Sadovaya Street, we find the Russian National Library, one of Russia's largest libraries with over 31 million items in its collection, and one of the most important sites of Russian cultural preservation in all of Russia. Called in tsarist times the "Imperial Public Library" and the "State Public Library" during the Soviet era, this magnificent institution, Russia's first public library, is still known by the nickname "Publichka." The core of the structure was built in the classical style from 1796 to 1801, though the library was not opened until 1814. In the years 1828–1834 the building received a new Rossi-designed facade and an extension with an impressive span of Ionic columns.

The opening of a railway line with Moscow in 1851 and the opening that year on Nevsky Prospect of the Nikolaevsky railway station—today known as the "Moscow Station," located at *ploshchad' Vosstaniia*, caused a dislocation in life on Nevsky Prospect. Petersburg, Schlögel writes, now was "no longer chiefly a street for parades and strolling, but instead had become a transportation artery, the setting for the ambivalence of progress and modernization." (Schlögel 164)

Gogol saw Petersburg, and indeed all of Russia, as an outsider, a provincial looking into the beautiful vetrine created by tsarist state under Peter, Catherine, and Nicholas, and by the cultural and social elites they fostered. His sense of alienation rings true to the experience of modern life.

CHAPTER FIVE

St. Petersburg
in the Creation
of Fyodor Dostoevsky

The writing of Fyodor Mikhailovich Dostoevsky is intimately associated with St. Petersburg. Over two-thirds of his collected novels and stories are set there. Perhaps the only other combinations of writer and city that rival in intensity are those of Balzac and Paris, Dickens and London, and Joyce and Dublin.

Dostoevsky was born in Moscow in 1821 and spent his childhood both there and on his father's estate in nearby Tula province. Fyodor's father, a former military physician and, at the time of his son's birth, the head of a hospital for the poor, was devout in his Orthodox faith. At the same time, however, he was emotionally unstable and often harsh with his children, as well as suspicious and stingy with those around him. Fyodor's mother was by all accounts a giving and gentle woman. When she died in 1837, Dostoevsky père sent his two sons, Fyodor and Mikhail, to a private school in Petersburg. The following year Fyodor passed the requisite examinations for admittance to the Academy of Engineering, where he was to be trained to be a military engineer. Dostoevsky had no interest in this profession, the study of which his father had arranged to ensure his son's future financial success.

The inner world of the young Dostoevsky had no place for the mundane existence of study at the academy. "My brother and I were then longing for a new life," he later wrote, recalling the Romantic inspiration he felt while a student. "We dreamt about something enormous, about everything 'beautiful and sublime'; such touching words were still fresh, and uttered without irony." (Frank 70) The harshly regimented, emotionally unfeeling life as a military engineer-in-training was not easy for the introspective, soul-searching Dostoevsky. He survived by reading voraciously, especially the German metaphysical Romantic poet Schiller and then later, the French social Romantic writers Balzac and Hugo. Before long, he determined for himself his future life's work. He wrote in a letter in 1839 that he aimed

> to study "the meaning of life and man" ... Man is an enigma. This enigma must be solved, and if you spend all your life at it, don't say you have wasted your time; I occupy myself with this enigma because I wish to be a man. (Frank 90–91)

Dostoevsky graduated from the academy in 1843; the next year he retired from his position in the state engineering service and set out to make his living as a writer.

The Academy of Engineering was housed in a former imperial palace, built for his own use by emperor Paul I, who reigned from 1796 to 1801, having assumed the throne at the death of his mother, Catherine the Great. Called then the Mikhailovsky Castle (it was even surrounded by a moat), the palace is located opposite the Summer Garden, across the Moika River. The building was completed in February 1801. Emotionally unstable, the unpredictable and martinet-like emperor was murdered here on the night of March 11–12, 1801, in a coup led by the Governor-General of Petersburg. As the place of a regicide, the imperial family did not want to keep the building, and it subsequently became the home of the Academy of Engineering, named after emperor Nicholas I, who was the son of

Paul, as was Nicholas's predecessor on the throne, Alexander I. Today, the building is used by restorers of the Russian Museum. Some of its rooms are open to the public, including several that are used as an art gallery, as well as the castle's chapel.

CITY AS PROTAGONIST

The city of Petersburg can be seen as Dostoevsky's most important protagonist, and this is amply borne out in the works that will be discussed in detail below. The districts frequented by proper society, wealthy citizens, and by government officials—indeed, the areas that tourists are most likely to visit today were of much less interest to Dostoevsky than the areas where the city's middle- and lower-class lived and worked. Dostoevsky was known to wander along the most out-of-the-way, forgotten streets of the city; here he saw the people he was interested in writing about. Nevsky Prospect, for instance, is not a significant locale in his writings. The most prominent area of the city in Dostoevsky's works is bounded by Voznesensky Street and Gorokhovaya Street, beyond the Moika River. Like Nevsky, these two streets radiate out from the Admiralty building toward the south and southwest, but in Dostoevsky's time they were decidedly more déclassé than the more famous Nevsky. The place of central interest in this triangle is the Haymarket (*Sennaia ploshchad'*), located along the Sadovaya Street between Voznesensky Prospect and Gorokhovaya Street. It is in the buildings and streets in the Haymarket district that the events of *Crime and Punishment* take place.

As the fifteen-year-old Dostoevsky made his way in 1837 to Petersburg from Moscow, that same symbolic journey from an old Russian world to a new one that Herzen would make two years later, he witnessed a sight while resting at a road-side that would shake him to his core. Years later, he recorded:

> Directly across the street from the inn was the station building. Suddenly a courier's troika came flying up to the station entrance and a government courier leapt out; ... The

courier was a tall, extremely stout, and strong fellow with a purplish face. He ran into the station and, no doubt, knocked back a glass of vodka there. I recall that our driver said that such couriers always drink a glass of vodka at every station, since without it they couldn't stand up to "the punishment they have to take." In the meantime a new troika of fresh, spirited horses rolled up to the station and the coachman, a young lad of twenty or so, wearing a red shirt and carrying his coat on his arm, jumped onto the seat. The courier at once flew out of the inn, ran down the steps, and got into the carriage. Before the coachman could even start the horses, the courier stood up and, silently, without any word whatsoever, raised his huge right fist and dealt a painful blow straight down on the back of the coachman's neck. The coachman jolted forward, raised his whip, and lashed the shaft horse with all his might. The horses started off with a rush, but this did nothing to appease the courier. He was not angry; he was acting according to his own plan, from something preconceived and tested through many years of experience; and the terrible fist was raised again, and again it struck the coachmen's neck, and then again and again; and so it continued until the troika disappeared from sight. Naturally the coachman, who could barely hold on because of the blows, kept lashing the horses every second like one gone mad; and at last his blows made the horses fly off as if possessed....

This disgusting scene has stayed in my memory all my life.... Every blow that rained down on the animal was the direct result of every blow that fell on the man. (Dostoevsky, *A Writer's Diary* 327–328)

In his magisterial, multi-volume biography of the writer, Joseph Frank argues that this event, the importance of which for Dostoevsky is also indicated by his reference to it in the notebooks he used for *Crime and Punishment*, shows that the young Dostoevsky did not see the world around him solely in terms dictated by the conventions of Romanticism. A realistic, hard-headed recognition of the messier side of life, to which the writer would be abundantly exposed in Petersburg, were central to his art.

Dostoevsky places a similar event near the beginning of *Crime and Punishment* in a dream of the protagonist, Raskolnikov. In the dream, Raskolnikov relives a scene he had witnessed as a boy (similarly, Dostoevsky's experience remained in his mind's eye throughout his life). A drunken peasant, Mikolka, emerges from a tavern, immediately becomes enraged at the old mare tied to his cart, and proceeds mercilessly to beat the horse to death. The sleeping Raskolnikov sees his younger self:

> [T]he poor boy is beside himself. With a shout he tears through the crowd to the gray horse, throws his arms around her dead, bleeding muzzle, and kisses it, kisses her eyes and mouth ... Then he suddenly jumps up and in a frenzy flies at Mikolka with his little fists. At this moment his father, who has been chasing after him all the while, finally seizes him and carries him out of the crowd.
>
> "Come along, come along now!" he says to him. "Let's go home!"
>
> "Papa! What did they ... kill ... the poor horse for!" he sobs, but his breath fails, and the words burst like cries from his straining chest. (Dostoevsky, *Crime and Punishment* 58–59)

This passage says much about the sense of guilt that Raskolnikov feels about the horrific deed of murder he is contemplating, but also about the pain and suffering of the Russian people. On the road to Petersburg as a boy, Dostoevsky saw a chain of suffering: horses being whipped by a driver who was himself being beaten by the courier. The parallel with Raskolnikov's murder of the old pawnbroker is obvious, with the implication that there is some cause beyond Raskolnikov himself, beyond his own soul, that bears some blame. The inhuman treatment of man by man, including the Russian state's oppression of its own subjects, is arguably this underlying factor. Dostoevsky is not interested in exculpating Raskolnikov; he did not hold to the literary school of naturalism, according to which, human actions are understood only as the inevitable product of natural causes and immutable laws inherent in the universe. On the other hand, Dostoevsky also does not deny the influence of environment on human actions. As the character Svidrigailov in *Crime and Punishment* argues:

> This is a city of half-crazy people. If we had any science, then physicians, lawyers, and philosophers could do the most valuable research on Petersburg, each in his own field. One seldom finds a place where there are so many gloomy, sharp, and strange influences on the soul of man as in Petersburg. (*Crime and Punishment* 267)

AS A REFLECTION OF CHARACTER
In the works of the mature Dostoevsky, Petersburg is not a sort of Petri dish where human actions are examined and explained, as they frequently are in the naturalist fiction of Émile Zola. In Dostoevsky's best writing, Petersburg is more than simply a social setting. It is a place where the physical attributes of the city reflect the inner world of his characters. This approach to Petersburg and its inhabitants grows organically out of the myth of Petersburg created by Pushkin and then further developed by Gogol, Dostoevsky's most immediate and significant influence among Russian writers.

While St. Petersburg is most evocatively rendered in *Crime and Punishment*, several earlier works set in the city deserve discussion here, as they help us to understand Dostoevsky's development as a writer and the position of Petersburg in his literary creation. Dostoevsky published his first novel, *Poor Folk*, in 1846. This short work, a novella actually, is what literary scholar Victor Terras and others call a "physiology" of a city—a study of a number of types of individuals that in writer's artistic vision help illustrate the overall state of health of the society depicted. This type of literary creation focused on the lower-class, particularly urban, population. The creations of both Balzac and Gogol influenced Dostoevsky greatly toward this sort of analysis in his own writing. The poet, critic, and journalist Nikolai Nekrasov (1821–1877) read the manuscript and then gave it to the enormously influential literary critic Vissarion Belinsky (1811–1848), saying, "a new Gogol has appeared!" (Fanger 162) Belinsky, who held that literature should champion social and political progress, was also impressed, and he heaped praise upon *Poor Folk*. This was immensely significant for Dostoevsky as it provided his breakthrough as a writer. Belinsky was more than an arbiter of literary taste, he was also a social critic whose views were followed by much of Russia's intelligentsia.

Just what did Dostoevsky glean from Gogol? "We all have come out from under Gogol's 'Overcoat'," Dostoevsky is said to have asserted. Not only did the two authors write primarily about Russia's urban lower- and as-yet-amorphous middle class, from déclassé aristocrats to persons on the verge of penury, such as Gogol's low-level civil servant, Akaky Akakievich. More importantly, Dostoevsky learned from his predecessor how comedy and tragedy are linked by the grotesque—an artistic vision that depicts persons and events that are absurd, fantastical, and even bizarre. From Gogol he learned that a writer could combine these literary modes to produce his own subjective view of his surroundings—his own aesthetic interpretation of Petersburg—that had enormous literary power. Professor Fanger elucidates:

> In Russia, Gogol's peculiar romantic realism led, by example and reaction, to the "fantastic realism," that "realism in a higher sense," of Dostoevsky, in which the comic ballast dropped away, the supernatural was rationalized, the essential ambiguity was given a philosophical basis, and the grotesque

and absurd—against the background of fantastic Petersburg—took on an existential starkness, a dark beauty, a new
and indisputable tragedy. (Fanger 125–126)

DOSTOEVSKY'S TRANSFORMATION

In 1849 Dostoevsky was arrested for his participation in an
illegal group of intellectuals that met to discuss political and
social ideas. Unifying the group was an attraction to utopian
socialism, though there was some advocacy of less revolutionary
reform of the oppressive Russian government under Nicholas
the I. The state took such talk seriously, and a number of the
group were executed and the rest imprisoned. After eight
months locked up in the Peter and Paul Fortress, across the
Neva from the Hermitage, Dostoevsky was placed before a
firing squad, and then spared at the last second. The mock exe-
cution, designed as part of his punishment, was followed by
four years of hard labor in Siberia and then five years as a sol-
dier. By the time he returned to Petersburg, in 1859, Dostoevsky's views of society and the individual's place within it had
undergone great change. No longer believing that mankind
could be changed through the social and political reforms advocated by the European left, Dostoevsky now held to a vision
focused on the moral and religious dimensions of the human
experience. This sea-change in outlook naturally had a profound impact on his art.

In 1864 Dostoevsky published *Notes from Underground*, a
complicated, satirical work exploring the existential condition
of mankind. His unnamed narrator, a retired minor civil servant, comments:

> Ordinary human consciousness would be too much for
> man's everyday needs, that is, half or a quarter of the
> amount which falls to the lot of a cultivated man of our
> unfortunate nineteenth century, especially one who has the
> particular misfortune to inhabit Petersburg, the most
> abstract and intentional city in the world. (There are

intentional and unintentional cities.) (Dostoevsky, *Notes from Underground* 6).

The criticism here of the "cultivated man of our unfortunate nineteenth century" is directed against those same utopian socialists with whom Dostoevsky had associated in the late 1840s. In this book Dostoevsky was responding to the writing of Nikolai Chernyshevsky (1828–1889), who believed that the rational pursuit of self-interest and productive labor would produce human happiness. Dostoevsky rejected the view that man's nature was controllable through social systems; instead, society could be bettered only through the individual's own moral development. A few lines before the above-cited passage, the narrator opines:

> I am told that the Petersburg climate is bad for me, and that with my paltry means it is very expensive to live in Petersburg. I know all that better than all these sage and experienced counselors and monitors. But I am going to stay in Petersburg. I will not leave Petersburg! I will not leave Petersburg because ... Bah, after all it does not matter in the least whether I leave or stay. (*Notes from Underground* 5–6)

Why will the narrator remain in this "most abstract and intentional city" if he dislikes it so much? The reason is that there is a convergence between Petersburg as an idea, as a conceptual notion, and the ideas that emanate from within the narrator. Dostoevsky would use this same literary device to great effect in *Crime and Punishment*. As Fanger explains:

> [S]imply, he belongs there, in this city formed unnaturally ... by the will of a man, on inhospitable ground, *in the service of an idea*. There is an ontological consonance between the "anti-city" built in violation of the natural laws of growth and this anti-hero divorced from life—perhaps even a case of cause and effect. (Fanger 182)

The Petersburg in which Dostoevsky's characters move and live often has an abstract quality about it; the details of the surroundings of his characters are described realistically—there are no human noses running around in uniform on Dostoevsky's pages as there are in Gogol's—but the city itself has a contingent, if not evanescent, quality to it. A mythical, fantastical view of Petersburg was rooted in Dostoevsky's own experience; it was the way he himself saw the city. In an 1861 published sketch, the kind known in the 19th century as a "feuilleton," Dostoevsky wrote:

I remember once on a wintry January evening I was hurrying home from the Vyborg side. I was still very young then. When I reached the Neva, I stopped for a minute and then threw a piercing glance along the river into the smoky, frostily dim distance, which had suddenly turned crimson with the last purple of a sunset that was dying out on the hazy horizon. Night lay over the city, and the whole immense plain of the Neva, swollen with frozen snow, under the last gleam of the sun, was strewn with infinite myriads of sparks of spindly hoar-frost. There was a twenty-degree frost ... Frozen steam poured from tired horses, from running people. The taut air quivered at the slightest sound, and columns of smoke like giants rose from all the roofs on both embankments and rushed upward through the cold sky, twining and untwining on the way, so that it seemed new buildings were rising above the old ones, a new city was forming in the air ... It seemed, finally, that this whole world with all its inhabitants, strong and weak, with all their domiciles, the shelters of the poor or gilded mansions, resembled at this twilight hour a fantastic, magic vision, a dream which would in its turn vanish immediately and rise up as steam toward the dark-blue sky. Some strange thought suddenly stirred in me. I shuddered, and my heart was as if flooded with a hot rush of blood that boiled up suddenly from the surge of a powerful but hitherto unknown sensation. I

Mariinsky Theater of Opera and Ballet

The Mariinsky Theater of Opera and Ballet, generally known in the West by its Soviet name, the Kirov, dates back to the mid-1800s. This ballet theater, more so even than Moscow's elite Bolshoi, has created some of the most famous international superstars of dance of all time. Vatslav Nizhinsky, Anna Pavlova, George Balanchine, Rudolph Nureyev, Mikhail Baryshnikov have all danced, or in Balanchine's case choreographed, with this St. Petersburg company.

In the pre-revolutionary era the theater received royal patronage and was indeed fit for a tsar, with a grand opera box opposite center stage for the emperor. Sparkling chandeliers over a sea of blue and gold, some 1,600 velvet-covered seats, ornate murals, a mirrored theater buffet with gleaming parquet floors ... the Mariinsky itself was a vision of splendor and opulence. All was nearly destroyed by fire during World War II, in the 900-day Siege of Leningrad. The theater was restored in 1944.

During the Soviet era tickets were often hard to come by, held for Communist Party functionaries or reserved for foreign tourist groups who would bring much-needed hard currency to the government-run theater. The Kirov's great dancers began exiting the stage, never to return, with defections to the West—Nureyev in Paris, Baryshnikov in Canada.

Then an era of stagnation concluded while a period of uncertainty took hold. The concept of benefactors and patronage grew slowly in the new Russia. But under the artistic direction and conducting of Valery Gergiev, a native of the Caucasus, the Mariinsky has blossomed to its former splendor and far beyond, with not only classics choreographed with new vigor, costuming, and set design, but also innovative contemporary dance and music now becoming part of the fabric of the renowned theater.

seemed to have understood something in that minute which had till then only been stirring in me, but was still uninterpreted; it was as if my eyes had been opened to something new, to a completely new world, unfamiliar to me and known only by certain obscure rumors, by certain mysterious signs. I suppose that my existence began from just that minute. (Fanger 149–150)

CRIME AND PUNISHMENT

Beginning with *Notes from Underground,* Dostoevsky's treatment of Petersburg, and indeed his entire oeuvre, entered a new phase, aesthetically more profound than the works that came before it. Dostoevsky had developed his own vision of Petersburg as a place where the landscape of the city merges with the landscape of the soul. He places his characters in concrete locales and circumstances, but in doing so he aims not to advocate how those circumstances should be changed. Instead, he seeks to depict all the more acutely how and why human beings behave the way they do. His subject is nothing less than the human heart and soul.

Dostoevsky's great novel *Crime and Punishment,* published in 1866, should be read by all who wish to be educated. Though set in a very specific time and place—St. Petersburg of the 1860s—the novel addresses many themes central to cultures of all times and places. Among these is the violation of taboos and the cost such action has for the individual as well as for society. At the heart of the novel is the murder of an elderly pawnbroker and her sister at the hands of a young, one-time university student, Rodion Raskolnikov, who rationalizes the deed on an argument from utility. The bulk of the novel is taken up by a psychological portrait of Raskolnikov and several acquaintances and family members with whom he interacts while moving along a path toward an understanding of his crime, which he may or may not reach, depending on the reader's interpretation of the end of the book. What interests Dostoevsky is not the legal ramifications of the murder, which some might see implied in the title of the novel in its standard English-language translation, but rather the *moral* consequences with which Raskolnikov must come to terms. That this is the case is clear from the Russian-language title of the work, *Prestuplenie i nakazanie*, for the word *prestuplenie* means not only "crime," but also "transgression," and "overstepping." Dostoevsky plumbs the depths of Raskolnikov's transgression against the moral laws of mankind, his intentional overstepping of the boundary that moral codes place on the individual and his rationalizations.

With the exception of the book's epilogue, which finds Raskolnikov and the former prostitute Sonya in Siberia, all of *Crime and Punishment* takes place in Petersburg. The city itself and the places Dostoevsky inserts his characters reflect the internal world of those characters. Raskolnikov, for instance, lives in a cramped, rented room in the Haymarket area, one of the poorer sections of Petersburg. At the beginning of the novel, the reader follows him as he leaves his apartment into the city:

> It was terribly hot out, and moreover it was close, crowded; lime, scaffolding, bricks, dust everywhere, and that special summer stench known so well to every Petersburger who cannot afford to rent a summer house—all at once these things unpleasantly shook the young man's already over-wrought nerves. (*Crime and Punishment* 4)

The concrete, real city, merges with world in the mind of Dostoevsky's protagonist, a process that becomes clearer as the novel progresses.

Of all Dostoevsky's novels, *Crime and Punishment* contains the most precise topographical descriptions. Dostoevsky was known to spend large amounts of time walking about Petersburg, especially the Haymarket area, a habit that he attaches to the novel's main character, Raskolnikov. His precise descriptions of the buildings in which the novel's characters live has enabled literary historians to surmise which buildings

Dostoevsky had in mind when writing the novel. Most of them are still standing today.

LOCALES OF *CRIME AND PUNISHMENT* AND OTHER NOVELS

Haymarket Square

From the city's early years in the first decades of the 18th century, the Haymarket was an untidy, chaotic place, where produce, firewood, cattle feed, and even cattle too were sold. As late as the mid-19th century, a significant portion of the products and services in Russian towns and cities were agrarian in nature (22 percent in the 1850s). (Mironov 444) At the time Dostoevsky wrote *Crime and Punishment*, the area around Haymarket Square was run-down and shabby, with many taverns and places of prostitution. In the square itself, merchants, peddlers of all kinds, and peasant farmers gathered to sell their wares. At every step one was confronted by the Russian *narod*, or common folk. An excellent description of life in the square is found in Part One, Chapter V:

> It was about nine o'clock when he walked through the Haymarket. All the merchants with tables or trays, in shops big and small, were locking up their establishments, removing or packing away their wares, and going home, as were their customers. Numbers of various traffickers and ragpickers of all sorts were crowding around the ground floor cookshops, in the dirty and stinking courtyards of the houses on the Haymarket, and more especially near the taverns. Raskolnikov liked these places most, as well as all the neighboring side streets, in his aimless wanderings. Here his rags attracted no supercilious attention, and one could go about dressed in anything without scandalizing people. Just at K——ny Lane, on the corner, a tradesman and a woman, his wife, had been selling their wares from two tables: thread, trimmings, cotton handkerchiefs, and so on. They, too, were heading home, but lingered, talking with a

woman acquaintance who had come up to them. (*Crime and Punishment* 60–61)

Visitors to the Haymarket today will find it much changed since Dostoevsky's time, as it has become a trendy, upscale place. Renovations on the subway station for the square, called by the Haymarket's name in Russian, Sennaya ploshchad', were completed in 2003.

Raskolnikov's minute garret room (described in the novel, significantly, as resembling a coffin in size) is located on *Stolyarny pereulok*, in the Haymarket district. (The novel gives the name of the street only as "S- pereulok.") Soviet literary historian V.E. Kholshennikov thus describes the buildings in the area in Dostoevsky's time:

> The rooms and inner courtyards were strikingly gloomy. Living space in the city was expensive, and owners of buildings with rooms let out for rent organized them so that not one square yard was wasted. Windows were found in the more expensive, spacious apartments, which also had proper main entrances. But behind the low-lying entrances with their claustrophobic archways, there opened up an entire system of crowded courtyards, deep, like wells, where the sun never penetrated. Steep and narrow stone stairways led to dark, dank apartments. Here lived the very poorest residents of the capital. In the floors that were underground and partially underground were often found small shops and taverns—particularly on the Haymarket and on Sadovaya Street in the direction of Voznesensky Prospect. (Dokusov 384–385)

Dostoevsky himself lived in this area as he wrote *Crime and Punishment*. From 1864 to 1867 he lived in the building that today carries the address 9 Kaznacheiskaya ulitsa. The building that Dostoevsky apparently had in mind as Raskolnikov's, 19 Grazhdanskaya ulitsa (Civic Street, called Srednaya

meshchanskaya ulitsa in the tsarist period), is extremely close to
that in which Doestoevsky lived. Both buildings have sides that
front onto the same street, *Stolyarni pereulok* (Carpenters' Lane).
In the world of the novel, Alyona Ivanovna, the old woman
whom Raskolnikov kills, lived near the Kokushin Bridge that
crosses the Griboedov Canal. Her building's address is 73 Griboedov Canal, as far as literary historians can tell, given the
description of the building and other details in the novel.
(Among these is that the pawnbroker's building is 730 paces
from Raskolnikov's.) Many other areas of the city are mentioned, such as in passages in which Raskolnikov makes his way
to Petersburg University, located on Vasilevsky Island. However,
Dostoevsky consistently gives the greatest detail in his descriptions of the Haymarket area.[2]

Voznesensky Prospect

Much of Dostoevsky's novel *The Insulted and the Injured,* published in 1861, the first written after his return from exile,
takes place in this area, noted for its minor merchants and artisans, including many of German extraction. (Recall the
German artisan, a locksmith, that figures in Gogol's story
"Nevsky Prospect".) In the tsarist period, Petersburg was home
to many peoples who were not Russian by ethnicity or language, including Poles, Finns, Swedes, Estonians, and others.
(In 1869, Russians made up just over 82 percent within the
population of 667,000.) The largest of the non-Russian groups
in Petersburg in the 19th century were the Germans, who in
1869 numbered about 45,000, or just under seven percent of
the city's population. (Shangina 26) Near the opening of *The
Insulted and the Injured,* the narrator describes one German-
owned shop on this street:

> The customers of this confectioner's shop were mostly Ger-
> mans. They gathered there from all parts of the Voznesensky
> Prospect, mostly heads of shops of various sorts: carpenters,
> bakers, painters, hatters, saddlers, all patriarchal people in

the German sense of the word. Altogether the patriarchal tradition was kept up at Müller's. Often the master of the shop joined some customer of his acquaintance and sat beside him at the table, when a certain amount of punch would be consumed. The dogs and small children of the household would sometimes come out to see the customers too, and the latter used to fondle both the children and the dogs. They all knew one another and had a respect for one another. And while the guests were absorbed in the perusal of the German newspapers, through the door leading to the shopkeeper's rooms came the tinkling of "Mein lieber Augustin," on a cracked piano played by the eldest daughter, a little German miss with flaxen curls, very much like a white mouse. The waltz was welcomed with pleasure. I used to go to Müller's at the beginning of every month to read the Russian magazines which were taken there. (Dostoevsky, *The Insulted and the Injured* 4)

Gorokhovaya Street

On this street, which one reaches by walking along Sadovaya Street away from Haymarket Square in the direction of Nevsky Prospect, lived one of the main protagonists in Dostoevsky's novel *The Idiot*, also set in Petersburg. Dostoevsky wrote this book while living in Europe; it was published in 1868. Perhaps the diminished role of Petersburg in this novel is explained by the simple fact that the author was not walking the streets of the city as he wrote it. The main character, the kind and seemingly slow-witted Prince Myshkin, knows Petersburg poorly, having just returned after living many years abroad. There is, however, a notable description of the home, on Gorokhovaya Street, of the character Rogozhin, a young scion of a traditional merchant clan, who has inherited a great deal of money. Like many descriptions in *Crime and Punishment*, the reader senses here the same fantastical Petersburg that so informs the earlier novel. Throughout the *The Idiot*, Rogozhin pursues the beautiful, but doomed Nastasya Filippovna, and Prince Myshkin becomes entwined in their lives. Myshkin approaches the building in which Rogozhin lives with some trepidation:

> He knew that the house was on Gorokhovaya Street, not far from Sadovaya Street, and he decided to go there, hoping that by the time he reached the place he would at last have made up his mind.
>
> As he came to the crossing of Gorokhovaya and Sadovaya he was surprised by his own extreme state of emotion; he had not expected that his heart would be pounding so hard. One house, no doubt, because of its peculiar appearance, attracted his attention from a distance, and the prince later remembered saying to himself, "That must be the house." With great curiosity he walked toward it to see if his conjecture had been correct; he felt that he would for some reason be particularly distressed if he had guessed right. It was a large, gloomy house of three stories, of no particular architectural style, and of a dirty green color. A few such houses, a very few, built at the end of the last century [18th century], are still standing almost unchanged in these streets of Petersburg (where everything changes so rapidly). They were built solidly with thick walls and very few windows; sometimes they windows on the ground floor have iron bars. More often than not there is a moneychanger's shop below. *The Skopets*[3] sitting in this shop rents an apartment upstairs. Outside and inside, everything about the house seems inhospitable and forbidding, as if everything about it was dissembling and guarding secrets; and it would be hard to explain why one has this impression from the very look of the house. Architectural lines have, of course, a secret of their own. These houses are occupied almost exclusively by tradespeople. On reaching the outer gate and noticing an inscription on it, the prince read, "The house of the hereditary burgess[4] Rogozhin." (Dostoevsky, *The Idiot* 224)

Dostoevsky Home-Museum

From the time of his return to Petersburg in 1859 from exile in Siberia to his death in 1881 from a pulmonary hemorrhage, Dostoevsky spent most of his time in Petersburg. (In the 1860s and 1870s he made a number of trips to Europe, once staying abroad for a span of four years.) He lived in a number of buildings in the city during his lifetime. The building in which he lived the final years of his life, where he wrote his final novel, *The Brothers Karamazov*, and in which he died, is 5 Kuznechnyi pereulok. (The nearest metro stations are Vladimirskaya and Dostoevskaya.) The rooms that the writer and his family called home have been turned into a museum and reconstructed to appear as they did when Dostoevsky lived there.

The artistic and intellectual achievement of *Crime and Punishment* makes it one of the greatest works of literature ever written. In it, Dostoevsky describes nothing less than mankind's search for meaning in the universe. Hence his books are considered core readings in existentialist thought. Petersburg for the novel's characters is the world itself, the physical realm in which they, and we, try to find meaning. Fanger writes:

> He presented for the first time the life of the city in all its sordidness—not simply to show what these conditions automatically did to people, as the naturalists would show, but to raise the problem of how, within them, sentient human beings might pursue the quest for dignity. And on a less literal level, he raised the chaotic city to the position of a symbol of the chaotic moral world of man, so that the contradictions of the second find their counterpart in the contrasts of the first. He showed, without abstraction, bare human consciousness striving in a world where there were few of the usual categories of normality, striving with a terrible and unsought freedom, isolated and rootless, together without community, to rediscover the conditions for "living life." (Fanger 211)

If some potential readers of Dostoevsky's great novels fear tackling them, thinking they will be overwhelmed with something resembling a philosophical treatise, they fortunately would be mistaken. The novels pulse with life, tracing the kinds of thoughts we all have, the fears we all wish we could avoid, and the mistakes to which we all are prone. The novels set in Petersburg also present a compelling vision of the city and are the zenith of the myth of Petersburg. Let us give Dostoevsky the final word with a passage from his 1875 novel, *The Adolescent.* Here Dostoevsky hints at the Christian belief in the physical resurrection of the body from death, which Dostoevsky held, and pays tribute to the compelling image of the Bronze Horseman—the dread and great tsar whose name this city carries:

> But let me note in passing that the Petersburg mornings, which may seem the bleakest on our whole planet, have for me a unique poetic quality of fantasy ... Hundreds of times, as I've walked through the Petersburg morning fog, this strange and clinging thought has cropped up: "What if, when the fog lifts and disperses somewhere high up over the earth, this rotten, slimy city is lifted up with it and vanishes like vapor until only the former Finnish marsh remains, and I suppose in the middle of it as a decoration, that bronze horseman on his panting, exhausted horse?" (Dostoevsky, *The Adolescent* 140)

CHAPTER SIX

Petersburg in the
Twentieth Century:
The City of Poets

The story of St. Petersburg in the 20th century is an exceedingly complicated one. Literature is perhaps one of the best resources for approaching life in the city throughout this tumultuous era in a way that breaks free of the conventional periodization determined by high politics. There were moments of promise and vigor, including the contradictory early years of the century, and a period in the 1920s. But for most of the century, literature was under siege, limited by an ideological straightjacket imposed by the USSR's Communist keepers. Most of the century was a tragic one for the city and its residents, with the nadir coming during the years of World War II. Petersburg was home to many of Russia's greatest poets in the twentieth century, and the fate of their home city occupied a primary place in their work.

To understand the position of Russian literature and writers at the outset of the new century, we must cast a glance back at the final years of the nineteenth century. This was a time not only of great artistic vibrancy, but also of rapid demographic expansion and economic development.

The population grew rapidly in the last decade of the

19th century and in the early 20th century; the city of some 670,000 in 1869 grew to 2.2 million in 1914, with most of this increase coming in the 1890s and in the 20th century. (Bater, *St. Petersburg: Industrialization and Change* 163, 308) Expansion of the urban industrial economy, especially in the form of large metalworking and textile factories, drew newcomers, primarily peasants, to the burgeoning Russian capital, though even more people were employed in the city's construction, transport, and service industries. Most of these workers lived in cramped and unhygienic apartments, their wages not high enough to afford anything else. In fact, in the early years of the new century, the cost of living was rising faster than were wages. Working hours were long: ten to twelve hours in factories, and as high as sixteen or even more for hired workers. Incredibly, some bakers worked as many as nineteen hours per day! (Hamm 50)

The social elite in Petersburg continued to consist primarily of those holding lofty rank either in the civil service or military. High culture was enjoyed by this group, who possessed the social inclination and education necessary to enjoy and participate in it, as well as the resources in time and money to do so. The city's middle class was growing, the result of expanding industry, banking, commercial and other economic sectors that are part of a modern economy characterized by growing entrepreneurship. But while in other cities, including Moscow, income level was increasingly the factor that determined one's social status, this was less the case in Petersburg. Moreover, the nature of the city's population growth meant that the proportion of residents who comprised educated society—nobles, bureaucrats, educated professionals (known as the "intelligentsia") and a few upwardly-mobile merchants—was ever shrinking, even though their overall numbers were growing.

For the city's peasant population—over 68 percent of the population as late as 1910—musical and theatrical performances with free admission were on occasion made available, though such entertainments were not as widely enjoyed as was drinking and other less than enlightening activities. (Hamm 65) Many among the city's poorer classes were not able to read; in 1897, only 74 percent of residents were literate. While this figure may seem low, it was higher than in the Russian population overall, and was higher than in the 1860s, despite the rise in the number of peasants in the intervening period. (Kovalchuk 288–289) The immense gulf between the majority population in Petersburg and the small cultural elite that read high fiction, must be borne in mind. This cultural gap continued into the Soviet period as well, though in time it was ameliorated, largely due to the affirmative action approach the Bolshevik leadership took towards the Russian working class.

There was great diversity in the literary life of fin-de-siècle Petersburg. The great age of the realist novel—the main representatives of which were Dostoevsky, Turgenev, and Tolstoy—had come to an end. However, a form of realism marked by materialism, utilitarianism and positivism remained influential. This aesthetic had spread in the 1860s and 1870s through the influence of the radical and revolutionary intelligentsia, who held that literature should be a tool for the improvement of society, primarily by wielding a critique of the social and political conditions in Russia, the true representatives of which the intelligentsia saw in the common Russian people.

The popularity of positivist and utilitarian views in Russia in the late 19th century can be traced to two influential writers: the journalist, author, and critic Nikolai Chernyshevsky (1829–1889) and Nikolai Nekrasov (1821–1877), a poet and journalist. While imprisoned in the Saints Peter and Paul Fortress in Petersburg in 1862 and 1863 under suspicion of engaging in revolutionary activities, Chernyshevsky wrote a socialist utopian novel titled *What Is To Be Done?* More Russians subsequently read this work than probably any other novel in the nineteenth century, though it strikes most readers today as didactic and boring. In Chernyshevsky's view, art's proper aims are utilitarian in nature: to convey information, encourage social progress, and be a "textbook for life," as he put it. (Terras

298) (Dostoevsky's novel *Notes from Underground* is a response to Chernyshevsky's novel.) Nekrasov purchased the journal *Sovremennik* ("The Contemporary") in 1846 and made it the chief voice of the radical intelligentsia in the 1850s and 1860s. Chernyshevsky worked as an editor for the journal for a period and it was here that his novel was published. Nekrasov's apartment on Liteiny Prospect 32 has been turned into a museum.

Beginning in the 1890s and continuing into the mid-1920s, an artistic and cultural revival occurred in Russia known as the "Silver Age," the first modernist movement in the arts in the country. The era was particularly known for its tremendous output in poetry. (The name "Silver Age" implicitly labeled the time of Pushkin as the "golden age.") Those who participated in the Silver Age and those profoundly influenced by it rejected the populism, materialism, and Marxism that formed the intellectual bedrock of most of educated Russian society in the preceding several decades, and turned instead to idealism and even religion.

The arrival of modernism in Russia can be dated to a lecture given in Petersburg on October 26, 1892 by the poet and critic Dmitry Merezhkovsky (1865–1941) titled "On The Reasons for the Decline and on New Trends in Contemporary Russian Literature." Merezhkovsky held that Russian literature needed an injection of new blood, in his words, "an expansion of artistic impressionability."[5] Russian writers, he said, should turn to contemporary European literature for models, particularly to the French decadent poets, and new consideration should be made of the Russian classics—Pushkin, and also the poets Tyutchev and Fet. Merezhkovsky's intellectual partner and wife, the poet Zinaida Gippius (1869–1945), were central figures in the development of Russian Symbolism. Art, for the Symbolists, was the means through which a more profound truth and reality could be found and expressed than was available through science and materialism. Symbolism's emphasis on an inner world of emotion and imagination as the true realm of human experience thus made it similar to Romanticism.

Merezhkovsky teamed with artist Alexander Benois and impresario Sergei Diaghilev in founding in Petersburg an illustrated journal, *Mir iskusstva* ("*World of Art*") through which they advocated their ideas for new artistic directions. The journal became immensely influential on artistic life not only in Petersburg but all of Russia. Benois later explained that the *Mir iskusstva* group pushed for a "departure from the backwardness of Russian artistic life, getting rid of our provincialism, and approaching the cultural West." (Volkov, *St. Petersburg* 476) Symbolism and the artistic movement that gathered around the *Mir iskusstua* journal was seen by the intelligentsia on the political left as an abandonment of the cause of social improvement and condemned it as "art for art's sake." The Symbolists for their part rejected the ideas that had motivated the intelligentsia of Chernyshevsky's and Nekrasov's day, believing that the creation of art and beauty, not social justice, would summon a rebirth for Russia. Philosopher Nikolai Berdyaev (1874–1948), who aligned himself with the Symbolist movement, later explained: "We saw the glow of a new dawn ... and the end of an old age seemed to coincide with a new era which would bring about a complete transfiguration of life." (George and George 377–378)

By the early years of the new century, Merezhkovsky and Gippius championed a messianic mixture of Christianity and Neoplatonic and Nietzschean thought. In 1901 they founded the Religious-Philosophical Society of St. Petersburg, which included important writers such as Andrei Bely, Alexander Blok, Fyodor Sologub, Vasily Rozanov, and others. But more influential than this society were gatherings at Merezhkovsky and Gippius's apartment, which thus doubling as a literary salon, was arguably the most important place in the Petersburg literary scene in the early 20th century. This apartment was in the "Muruzy House," located on the corner of Liteiny Prospect and Panteleimonovskaya Street, and named after the building's owner. Except for the period 1906–1908, when Merezhkovsky and Gippius lived in Paris, established writers, and those who sought to become known as writers, regularly gathered here on late Sunday evenings until the pair fled Russia after the 1917 Revolution. A tall, imperious woman who wielded her sensuality like a weapon, Gippius ran the salon, while the shy Merezhkovsky often stayed in a back room to read and write. The assessments of a fledgling writer's work from Gippius, known as the "Decadent Madonna," could help make or break a career.

ALEXANDER BLOK

While the Symbolists in the 1890s were seen as a group of eccentrics, in the early twentieth century they became hugely popular, and their views replaced the utilitarianism of Chernyshevsky to represent the dominant literary mode. Easily the best and most popular of the Symbolist writers was the lyric poet Alexander Blok (1880–1921), whose personal popularity among the Petersburg reading public reached cult-like levels in the early twentieth century. A mystical dualism is strongly borne out in Blok's verse: dream and reality, this world and other worlds. In Blok, the metaphysical is found through and within the ordinary.

Blok had studied law at St. Petersburg University, but after being introduced to the theater and then poetry he radically changed the course of his studies; he completed a degree in the humanities in 1906, after he already was an established poet. Primary influences upon his verse were Pushkin and the Orthodox mystic and symbolist philosopher Vladimir Solovyov. One of Blok's innovations as a Symbolist was the attention he paid to the urban lower classes. However, Blok's sensibility was entirely different from that of the left intelligentsia in earlier decades, his verse being highly impressionistic, very rhythmical and musical. Unfortunately, these latter qualities are generally lost in translation. For Blok, music was part of his aesthetic vision; in 1919 he recorded in his diary:

> In the beginning there was music. Music is the essence of the world. The world grows in elastic rhythms. This growth may

be contained for some time, only to burst forth in a flood. (Terras 393)

For instance, in the first stanza of Blok's poem "The Factory," written in 1903, most of the vowels are O's, representing the groans of workers, their backs bent with heavy sacks. Here are just the first two stanzas:

Next door the windows are yellow.
As the night falls, as the night falls
the pensive bolt creaks and the people
come up to the gates in the wall.

The gates are shut holding them back,
but on the wall, but on the wall
someone motionless, someone black
is silently counting them all. (Blok 46)

Petersburg appears prominently in Blok's poetic creation. For instance, a poem written in May 1901 within the poem cycle "Verses to the Beautiful Lady" contains the following lines displaying the colors with which Blok so often imbued his poetic descriptions of his home city:

By the white night, the red moon
Floats out in the blue.
It wanders, in spectral beauty,
Reflecting in the Neva.[6]

Between 1904 and 1908 Blok wrote a poem cycle titled "The City," in which he describes a Petersburg poised on the brink of apocalyptic destruction. The cycle includes several poems Blok wrote under the spell of Falconet's statue of Peter the Great. In one poem, written in February 1904, Peter spreads throughout the city a burning fire; in the final stanza, however, he shows himself to be the city's protector:

He will care after his city,
And, reddening before the dawn,
In his outstretched hand, his sword bursts into flame
Above the quietening capital.[7]

A poem written the next year, in October 1905, clearly bears
out the influence of the 1905 Revolution. Blok participated in
street demonstrations in 1905; his aunt recorded the instance of
one protest, at which the poet "carried at the head of it a red
flag, feeling himself at one with the crowd." (Kisch 46) Blok
hoped a new world would emerge out of the revolution, a hope
that rose in him again during the revolutionary year of 1917.

Suspended over the universal city,
Imprisoned in the dust of the past,
The monarch on a lyrical morning
Is still bowed down by omnipotent sleep.

His royal ancestor on bronze charger
Still rears, as ever, above the serpent,
And the many-stringed voices of the mob
Does not yet hold power on the Neva.

Over the houses flags already wave,
New nestlings are ready for the task;
Neva's limpid stream flows gently,
And blindness possesses the dark's palace.

If the face of liberty has been seen,
Yet first was seen the face of the serpent,
And not one joint has been crushed
Of the coils of its gleaming scales. (Kisch 47)

In both Peter poems, that of 1904 and 1905, Blok refers to a
malevolent "snake," which must be defeated, just as the horse
on which Falconet's Peter rides tramples a snake beneath its

hooves. In the later poem, certainly, the snake seems to represent the tsarist autocracy, the "dust of the past," that is holding back those who would establish a new "power on the Neva."

Blok greeted the Bolshevik Revolution with enthusiasm, seeing in it the chance for Russia's redemption. In his masterwork, *The Twelve*, written in January 1918, Blok combines explicit religious imagery with revolutionary violence to express the exhilaration and hope felt in the fall of 1917 by the lower classes in the city and by many members of the intelligentsia. While not religious himself in any conventional way, Blok saw a convergence between the ecstatic devotion to revolution maintained by many in Russia and the mystical sense of renewal present in religious feeling. In this poem, twelve Red Army soldiers march down the city streets in an engulfing blizzard, wreaking destruction as they go, as if doing away with the old Russia. The number of soldiers parallels the number of Jesus's apostles, and individual soldiers bear apostolic names. The poem's secular setting and religious imagery ends in a final, stunning apotheosis. Here is a selection from the last two of the poem's twelve sections:

> Abusing God's name as they go,
> all twelve march onward into snow ...
> prepared for anything,
> regretting nothing ...
>
> Their rifles at the ready
> for the unseen enemy
> in back streets, side roads
> where only snow explodes
> its shrapnel, and through quag-
> mire drifts where the boots drag ...
>
> before their eyes
> throbs a red flag.

Left, right,
the echo replies.

Keep your eyes skinned
lest the enemy strike!

Into their faces day and night
bellows the wind
without a break ...

Forward, and forward again
the working men!

... On they march with sovereign tread ...
Who else goes there? Come out! I said
come out! It is the wind and the red
flag plunging gaily at their head.
...
Who's that waving the red flag?
Try and see! It's as dark as the tomb!
Who's that moving at a jog
trot, keeping to the back-street gloom?

Don't you worry—I'll catch you yet;
better surrender to me alive!
Come out, comrade, or you'll regret
it—we'll fire when I've counted five!

Crack—crack—crack! But only the echo
answers from among the eaves ...
The blizzard splits his seams, the snow
laughs wildly up the whirlwind's sleeve ...

Crack—crack—crack!
Crack—crack—crack!

... So they march with sovereign tread ...
Behind them limps the hungry dog,
and wrapped in wild snow at their head
carrying a blood-red flag—
soft-footed where the blizzard swirls,
invulnerable where bullets crossed—
crowned with a crown of snowflake pearls,
a flowery diadem of frost,
ahead of them goes Jesus Christ. (Blok 157–160)

This transformative vision of both the common Russian people and of St. Petersburg was the climax of longings that Blok had long harbored. Years before he had written to Zinaida Gippius of a "New Petersburg city, coming out of heaven," which together with the mythic and magical Russian city of Kitezh "will be transformed on the last day." (Hackel 151) Victor Terras explains:

Blok believed that the bloodshed and suffering caused by the revolution were a necessary sacrificial offering to redeem the sins of Russia's past and that Russia would arise from its horrors purified. (Terras 431)

Blok later became severely disenchanted with the Bolsheviks, who saw little need of poetry in their attempt to build a new Russia. The early death of the poet, in 1921, spared him the enormous, and even murderous, pressure which the Soviet state would soon wield against Russia's most honest and talented writers, including the Petersburg poets Osip Mandelstam and Anna Akhmatova.

The apartment Blok lived in during the years 1899 to 1906 is the location of a literary museum to the poet. It is located on Dekabristov Street 57. Here one can view photos of Blok and mementos from his life, and one room has been restored to appear as it would have when the poet lived there.

ANDREI BELY

While Andrei Bely (1880–1934) was known by his contemporaries as an important Symbolist poet, he is remembered today primarily for his novel *Petersburg*, first published in 1913–1914, and then, with changes, in 1922. It is not a conventional novel in its composition, but rather a Symbolist poem in prose form that uses stream-of-consciousness techniques. The slender plot, set in the city in 1905, involves a university student who promises a group of revolutionaries that, using a bomb they have supplied, he will blow up his father, a high-level state bureaucrat. While Bely was more associated with literary circles in Moscow than in Petersburg, his novel is considered to be one of the primary contributions to the literary image and myth of Petersburg. Vladimir Nabokov held the novel in the same high regard he did the other great modernist works *Ulysses*, by James Joyce, Kafka's *The Metamorphosis*, and Proust's *Remembrance of Things Past*.

Early in the novel Bely describes the mingling of the worlds of the working-class districts with the central areas of the city and the growing revolutionary pressures that he sensed in the early 20th century:

Petersburg is surrounded by a ring of many-chimneyed factories.

A many-thousand swarm plods towards them in the morning, and the suburbs are all aswarm. All the factories were then in a state of terrible unrest. The workers had turned into prating shady types. Amidst them circulated Brownings. And then something else again.

The agitation that ringed Petersburg then began penetrating even to the very centers of Petersburg. It first seized the islands, then crossed the Liteiny and Nikolaevsky Bridges. On Nevsky Prospect circulated a human myriapod. However, the composition of the myriapod kept changing; and an observer could now note the appearance of a shaggy black fur hat from the fields of bloodstained Manchuria.

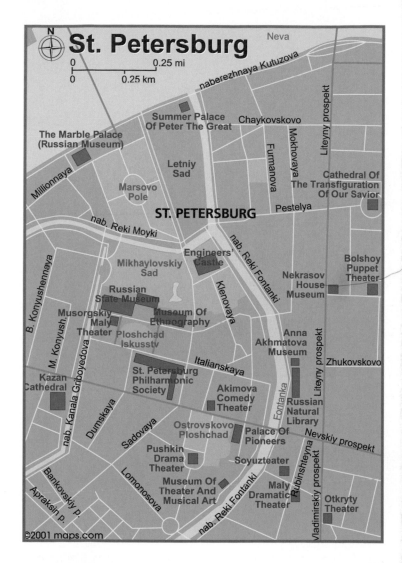

N

St. Petersburg

Neva

0   0.25 mi

0   0.25 km

naberezhnaya Kutuzova

Summer Palace Of Peter The Great

Chaykovskovo

The Marble Palace (Russian Museum)

Mokhovaya

Furmanova

Liteyny prospekt

Letniy Sad

Cathedral Of The Transfiguration Of Our Savior

Millionnaya

Marsovo Pole

ST. PETERSBURG

Pestelya

nab. Reki Moyki

Engineers' Castle

nab. Reki Fontanki

Mikhaylovskiy Sad

Nekrasov House Museum

Bolshoy Puppet Theater

Russian State Museum

Klenovaya

B. Konyushennaya

Musorgskiy Maly Theater

Museum Of Ethnography

Anna Akhmatova Museum

Liteyny prospekt

Zhukovskovo

M. Konyush

Ploshchad Iskusstv

St. Petersburg Philharmonic Society

Italianskaya

Kazan Cathedral

nab. Kanala Griboyedova

Dumskaya

Akimova Comedy Theater

Fontanka

Russian Natural Library

Ostrovskovo Ploshchad

Palace Of Pioneers

Nevskiy prospekt

Sadovaya

Pushkin Drama Theater

Soyuzteater

Rubinshteyna prospekt

Bankovskiy p.

Lomonosova

Museum Of Theater And Musical Art

Maly Dramatic Theater

Otkryty Theater

Apraksin p.

nab. Reki Fontanki

Vladimirskiy prospekt

©2001 maps.com

■ Shown above is a city map of St. Petersburg, which was founded in the early 1700s by Tsar Peter the Great. Built along the Neva River, the area has been an important transportation and trade location since the 9th century. By 1712, Tsar Peter had built St. Petersburg into Russia's new capital city.

■ Peter ascended the throne at the age of ten, ruling jointly with his brother Ivan. After his brother's death, Peter the Great, pictured above, began making huge reforms in Russia. He is credited with modernizing Russia and reforming the country to compete with European powers of the time.

■ The Winter Palace along the Neva River, shown here, is one of St. Petersburg's most beautiful examples of Baroque architecture. The palace was built between 1754 and 1762 for Empress Elizabeth, Peter the Great's daughter. Today, the palace houses the Hermitage Museum, one of the world's most prestigious art galleries.

■ The Bronze Horseman statue above shows Peter the Great in Senatskaia Ploshchad (Square). The monument was commissioned by German-born Empress Catherine the Great as a tribute to Russian culture and as a means of establishing her relationship with Russian heritage.

■ This is a portrait of 19th century writer Alexander Pushkin, credited with being the founder of modern Russian literature. Pushkin was the first to blend Old Slavonic and vernacular language to create a new genre of modern poetry.

■ Built between 1714 and 1725, Peterhof, above, includes a palace, fountains, and parks. Located outside the city of St. Petersburg, Peterhof was built by famous architects, folk craftsmen, and anonymous designers.

■ Nikolai Vasilevich Gogol is among the most influential of Russian writers. Gogol moved to St. Petersburg in 1828 and traveled extensively while writing. His publications include *Evenings on a Farm near Dikanka* (1831), "The Nose" (1836), and *Dead Souls* (1842).

■ The above portrait shows Fyodor Dostoevsky, a renowned Russian writer forever associated with the city of St. Petersburg. Famous for his look into the darker side of the human psyche, *Crime and Punishment* is the novel in which Dostoevsky first develops the theme of redemption through suffering, which would reappear throughout his later works.

■ Maxim Gorky, meaning "the bitter one," changed his name from Aleksey Maksimovich Peshkov to reflect his abusive and neglected childhood. Gorky, shown here, is working on one of his many plays, for which he gained national recognition.

■ Pictured here is one of Russia's greatest poets, Anna Akhmatova. Her works are considered feminine and honest, but the Soviets banned them for their lack of optimism.

■ Above is the Church of the Savior on the Spilled Blood, or just Church on the Blood. It is here where Alexander II was fatally wounded in an assassination attempt in 1881. The church was designed in the older style of Russian churches, contrasting the surrounding Baroque and Classical architecture.

There was a sharp drop in the percentage of passing top hats. Now were heard the disturbing antigovernment cries of street urchins running at full tilt from the railway station to the Admiralty waving gutter rags.

Those were foggy days, strange days. Noxious October marched on. Dust whirled through the city in dun brown vortexes, and the rustling crimson fell submissively at the feet to wind and chase at the feet, and whitish, plaiting yellow-red scatterings of words from leaves.

Such were the days. Have you ever slipped off at night into the vacant plots of city outskirts to hear the same importunate note "oo"? Oooo-oooo-ooo: such was the sound in that space. But was it a sound? It was the sound of some other world. And it attained a rare strength and clarity. "Ooo-oooo-ooo" sounded softly in the suburban fields of Moscow, Petersburg, Saratov. But no factory whistle blew; there was no wind; and the dogs remained silent. (Bely 52)

Bely's poetic novel abounds in textual examples of the myth of Petersburg—a blend of mirage and illusion with stones, bricks, canals, and palaces. Petersburg's status as both literary symbol and physical city is made clear in the Prologue:

Nevsky Prospect is a prospect of no small importance in this un-Russian—but nonetheless—capital city. Other Russian cities are a wooden heap of hovels.

And strikingly different from them all is Petersburg.

. . .

[I]f Petersburg is not the capital, then there is no Petersburg. It only appears to exist.

However that may be, Petersburg not only appears to us, but actually does appear—on maps: in the form of two small circles, one set inside the other, with a black dot in the center; and from precisely this mathematical point, which has no dimension, it proclaims forcefully that it exists: from here, from this very point surges and swarms

Vladimir Nabokov

The Russian-American writer Vladimir Vladimirovich Nabokov (1899–1977) was born in Petersburg, in the house at 47 *Bol'shaya morskaya ulitsa*, not far from St. Isaac's Cathedral. His family was wealthy, of nobility status, and had a distinguished record of government and public service. The writer's grandfather, Dmitry Nikolaevich Nabokov, was Russia's Minister of Justice from 1878 to 1885, and his paternal grandmother, Maria von Korff, was a German baroness. Their son, and the writer's father, Vladimir Dmitrievich Nabokov, was also a jurist.

The Nabokov household was strongly Anglophile; Vladimir Nabokov could write in English before he could in Russian. (He also became fluent in French as a boy.) After being tutored at home, the young Nabokov attended a prestigious, innovative Petersburg school. He later recorded his impressions of the city in winter, remembering "those exiting St Petersburg mornings when the fierce and tender, damp and dazzling arctic spring bundled away broken ice down the sea-bright Neva! It made the roofs shine. It painted the slush in the streets a rich purplish-blue shade which I have never seen anywhere since." (Nabokov 83). He also wrote colorfully of the drive (by automobile) from his home to school: "Upon reaching Nevski Avenue, one followed it for a long stretch, during which it was a pleasure to overtake with no effort some cloaked guardsman in his light sleigh drawn by a pair of black stallions snorting and speeding along under the bright blue netting that prevented lumps of hard snow from flying into the passenger's face. A street on the left side with a lovely name—Karavannaya (the Street of the Caravans)—took one past an unforgettable toyshop. Next came the Cinizelli Circus (famous for its wrestling tournaments). Finally, after crossing an ice-bound canal one drove up to the gates of Tenishev School in Mohovaya Street (the Street of Mosses)." (Nabokov 142) the printed book; from this invisible point speeds the official circular. (Bely 2)

OSIP MANDELSTAM

Petersburg figures prominently in the verse of Osip Mandelstam, widely considered to be one of the world's finest poets of the twentieth century. Mandelstam's interest in the city focused upon its prominent squares, imposing government buildings, and the large churches that are so characteristic of the area near the beginning of Nevsky Prospect and along the nearby banks of the Neva.

Mandelstam was born in 1891 in Warsaw, not Petersburg, but at a very young age he moved with his family to the imperial capital, which he soon came to consider his native city. Mandelstam belonged to an artistic and aesthetic school known as Acmeism, a child of the Symbolist school. Like the Symbolists, Acmeists also held to an idealist (non-materialist) view of the world and the artist. But while Symbolists were influenced by European (particularly German) Romanticism and inclined toward mysticism, Acmeists were more interested in classical forms, and they rejected effusive emotionalism. The classical world, in their view, was a civilization whose power could extend to other parts of the earth, enlivening and enriching them. This view of art as unbounded by a given culture and language was typical of Acmeist thought. When once asked to define Acmeism, Mandelstam responded, "nostalgia for a world culture."

The Symbolists tended to see urban life, and thus Petersburg, as a threat to the purity of the human spirit. For the Acmeists, however, mankind's creations are not grotesque, but instead are filled with admirable order; they coexist, and even compete, with nature. (Terras 439–440) Mandelstam presents a beautiful interplay between the handiwork of both man and nature in his 1913 poem, "The Admiralty." To understand the Petersburg imagery in the poem, one must recall that the Admiralty building can be seen as one looks toward the Neva along any of the three thoroughfares that radiate from it

toward the southwest: Nevsky Prospect, Gorokhovaya Street, or
Voznesensky Street.

> The northern capital, a poplar tree droops, dusty,
> a transparent clock-dial tangled in leaves,
> and through dark foliage a frigate, an acropolis
> shines in the distance, brother to water, brother to sky.
>
> An air-boat, a mast no one can touch,
> a measure for Peter's heirs,
> and his lesson: a demigod's whim is not beauty,
> but the predatory eye of a carpenter, is.
>
> Four elements united, rule us, are friendly,
> but free man made the fifth.
> This chaste-constructed ark: isn't the
> superiority of space denied?
>
> Capricious jellyfish cling, angry;
> anchors rot, abandoned like ploughs—
> and there, the three dimensions burst their bounds
> and universal oceans open. (Mandelstam, *Complete Poetry
> of Osip Emilevich Mandelstam* 58)

In a perceptive essay on Mandelstam, the Nobel prize-win-
ning Russian poet Joseph Brodsky wrote that his predecessor's
identification with the Hellenic and Roman worlds was centered in a search for civilization amid the mélange of influences
that was the tsarist Russian empire. Early 20th-century Petersburg, Brodsky explains, was for Mandelstam both the focal
point and the material for this search, and the Admiralty was a
symbol of the kind of culture Mandelstam valued. Brodsky's
remarks are worth quoting here at length:

> The mediastinum of this Russian Hellenicism was St. Peters-
> burg. Perhaps the best emblem for Mandelstam's attitude

toward this so-called world culture could be that strictly classical portico of the St. Petersburg Admiralty decorated with reliefs of trumpeting angels and topped with a golden spire bearing a silhouette of a clipper at its tip. In order to understand his poetry better, the English-speaking reader perhaps ought to realize that Mandelstam was a Jew who was living in the capital of Imperial Russia, whose dominant religion was Orthodoxy, whose political structure was inherently Byzantine, and whose alphabet had been devised by two Greek monks. Historically speaking, this organic blend was most strongly felt in Petersburg, which became Mandelstam's "familiar as tears" eschatological niche for the rest of his not-that-long life.

It was long enough, however, to immortalize this place, and if his poetry is sometimes called "Petersburgian," there is more than one reason to consider this definition both accurate and complimentary. Accurate because, apart from being the administrative capital of the empire, Petersburg was also the spiritual center of it, and in the beginning of the century the strands of that current were merging there the way they do in Mandelstam's poems. Complimentary because both poet and the city profited in meaning by their confrontation. If the West was Athens, Petersburg in the teens of this century was Alexandria. This "window on Europe," as Petersburg was called by some gentle souls of the Enlightenment, this "most invented city," as it was defined later by Dostoevsky, lying at the latitude of Vancouver, in the mouth of a river as wide as the Hudson between Manhattan and New Jersey, was and is beautiful with that kind of beauty which happens to be caused by madness—or which tries to conceal this madness. Classicism never had so much room, and the Italian architects who kept being invited by successive Russian monarchs understood this all too well. The giant, infinite, vertical rafts of white columns from the façades of the embankments' palaces belonging to the Czar, his family, the aristocracy, embassies, and the *nouveaux riches* are carried by the reflecting river down to the Baltic. On the main avenue of the empire—Nevsky Prospect—there are churches of all creeds. The endless, wide streets are filled with cabriolets, newly introduced automobiles, idle, well-dressed crowds, first-class boutiques, confectionaries, etc. Immensely wide squares with mounted statues of previous rulers and triumphal columns taller than Nelson's. Lots of publishing houses, magazines, newspapers, political parties (more than in contemporary America), theaters, restaurants, gypsies. All this is surrounded by the brick Birnam Wood of the factories' smoking chimneys and covered by the damp, gray, widespread blanket of the Northern Hemisphere's sky. One war is lost, another—a world war—is impending, and you are a little Jewish boy with a heart full of Russian iambic pentameters. (Brodsky, *Less than One: Selected Essays* 130–132)

After the Bolshevik Revolution, Mandelstam's view of Petersburg changed. The poet found life under the new regime to be oppressive and alienating. His deep nostalgia for pre-Soviet Petersburg is clearly borne out in a poem he wrote in 1920. Here are the first two plaintive stanzas:

> In Petersburg we'll meet again
> As though it was where we'd laid the sun to rest
> And there we'll utter one first time
> The word that's senseless but blessed.
> In the black velvet of the Soviet night,
> In the velvet of the universal void,
> The beloved eyes of the blesséd women still sing
> And immortal flowers still bloom.
>
> The wildcat capital arches its back,
> On the bridge a sentinel stands watch.
> Only a cuckoo car horn blares,
> Through the dark its angry engine roars.
> I don't need a permit for the night:
> Sentinels don't frighten me;

For the senseless and blessèd word
I shall pray in the Soviet night. (Mandelstam, *50 Poems* 51)

When this poem was written, the city had been known as "Petrograd" for several years. With the outbreak of war with Germany in 1914, it was felt that the more Slavic name was an improvement upon "Sankt-Peterburg," a name that sounded German, though it was actually Dutch in origin. (Peter the Great had learned shipbuilding in Holland in the late seventeenth century and was inspired by Amsterdam in his building of his new capital.) After Lenin's death in 1924, the city was renamed yet again, becoming "Leningrad" in honor of the Soviet leader. Mandelstam always felt that tsarist-era Petersburg was his home, and the later manifestations of the city seemed increasingly foreign to him. His close friend and fellow Acmeist poet Anna Akhmatova said of Mandelstam: "He became the last describer of life in Petersburg."[8]

Mandelstam published actively as a poet until 1928. As a result of the tightening ideological strictures of Soviet culture under Stalin, Mandelstam was able to publish very little after that date, and his last published poem appeared in 1932. In 1933 he read to a small group a satirical poem in which he referred to Stalin in a derogatory manner and was critical of life under his rule. One of those present denounced the poet to the authorities, and several months later Mandelstam was arrested and given a three-year sentence of exile in the city of Voronezh in south Russia. He was released in 1937, but the next year was arrested again in another of Stalin's murderous purges. Mandelstam died in a prison camp in the Soviet Far East in 1938.

In a 1930 poem written upon returning to (now) Leningrad after an eight-month stay in Armenia, Mandelstam wrote this simple and prophetic poem:

Leningrad
I returned to my city, familiar as tears.
As veins, as mumps from childhood years.

You've returned here, so swallow as quick as you can
The cod-liver oil of Leningrad's riverside lamps.

Recognize when you can December's brief day:
Egg yolk folded into its ominous tar.

Petersburg, I don't yet want to die:
You have the numbers of my telephones.

Petersburg, I have addresses still
Where I can raise the voices of the dead.

I live on the backstairs and the doorbell buzz
Strikes me in the temple and tears at my flesh.

And all night long I await those dear guests of yours,
Rattling, like manacles, the chains on the doors.
    (Mandelstam, *50 Poems* 69)

Mandelstam now sees himself as a stranger in Leningrad, where so many of his friends are dead. Like countless others in the 1930s—artists, writers, and political opponents of Stalin— Mandelstam waits for the ring of the doorbell in the night, the usual time for the NKVD (secret police, predecessor of the KGB) to make arrests. In the following short poem written just one month later, Mandelstam's fears are palpable, and, tragically as we have seen, completely justifiable:

Succor me, O Lord, to live through this night:
I fear for my life, for Your handmaid—
to live in Petersburg's like sleeping in a coffin.
    (Mandelstam, *Poems from Mandelstam* 97)

ANNA AKHMATOVA
The life and work of Anna Akhmatova (1889–1966) is more closely associated with Petersburg than even that of Blok or

Mikhail Zoshchenko

Perhaps no other writer captured the dichotomy of Soviet life, in all its absurdities and contradictions, as well as Mikhail Zoshchenko. The writer first studied law in St. Petersburg, though he did not graduate with a degree in the field. Instead, he became one of the country's most widely read writers in the 1920s.

His early stories were devoted to his experiences in World War I and the Russian Civil War. He fought with the Bolsheviks, against the "Whites" or the Mensheviks. In the 1920s Zoshchenko joined a literary group known as the Serapion Brothers, devoted to being non-conformist, and inspired by the work of Yevgeny Zamyatin.

But eventually, when faced with the growing idiosyncrasies within the developing Soviet system, Zoshchenko began pointing them out in satirical tales of communal apartment living, food shortages, and other societal ills. While the author never directly attacked the Soviet system, his humorous short stories targeted problems of bureaucracy, corruption, poor housing, and shortages of consumer goods.

For those who remember the last days of the Soviet Union, Zoshchenko's tales rang true even then, some 60 years after he wrote them.

The author did indeed experience pressure to comply with Socialist Realism in his writings, and his autobiographical story "Before Sunrise" was banned in 1943. He was also expelled from the Soviet Writers' Union. Today Zoshchenko's works are still superbly entertaining, and provide a deep understanding of the way a great many people dealt with the harsh realities of Soviet life.

Mandelstam. Though Born in Odessa, where her father was serving in the navy, Akhmatova spent most of her life in Petersburg, to which she was fiercely devoted. Her early poetry bears a Symbolist influence, but in 1913 she joined with Mandelstam and Nikolai Gumilev, whom she had married in 1910, to form the Acmeist group of poets.

Akhmatova's verse is deeply lyrical, and each poem expresses a particular mood in a set time and place. Hers is a distinctly feminine voice, with a diction simpler than that of Mandelstam. She published several collections of poetry before the 1917 Revolution, but her primary contribution was made in the Soviet period, when her poetic voice of emotional and artistic honesty became revered throughout the country. With her artistic vision formed in the pre-Soviet era, she was always a Russian, never a Soviet, poet.

With the advent of the Soviet regime, Akhmatova sensed, as did Mandelstam, that Petersburg, and all of Russia, was entering a new dark age. In her poem "Petrograd, 1919" Akhmatova expresses anxiety that perhaps she and others were placing their love for Petersburg above the broader needs of Russia, then in the throes of the Civil War between Red and White military forces. The poet also asks whether the fervent attachment to Petersburg has left her and those like her without a place in the new, Bolshevik-controlled Russia:

> And confined to this savage capital,
> We have forgotten forever
> The lakes, the steppes, the towns,
> And the dawns of our great native land.
> Day and night in the bloody circle
> A brutal langour overcomes us ...
> No one wants to help us
> Because we stayed home,
> Because, loving our city
> And not winged freedom,
> We preserved for ourselves

Its palaces, its fire and water.
A different time is drawing near,
The wind of death already chills the heart,
But the holy city of Peter
Will be our unintended monument. (Akhmatova 259)

Akhmatova had great difficulty publishing her poetry beginning in the early 1920s, as the state authorities considered it
ideologically suspect. A collection appeared in 1940, and she
published some forgettable patriotic verse during World War II,
but by 1946 Soviet authorities were again condemning her verse
as "suffused with the spirit of pessimism, decadence ... and
bourgeois-aristocratic aestheticism."(Hosking 527) Stalin's ven-
omous commissar of culture, Andrei Zhdanov, denounced
Akhmatova as a "nun-whore."
     One of the seemingly paradoxical aspects of artistic and
intellectual life in the Soviet Union was that more often than
not, the greatest artists and thinkers were considered nobodies
by the state, through which all employment, housing, trav-
eling privileges, were channeled. However, this did not pre-
vent friends and close acquaintances from passing among
themselves copies of poetry and prose, duplicated using a
typewriter and carbon paper, or even simply hand-written.
This method of distribution and quasi-publication was known
as *samizdat*, which means, "self-publishing." Thus, while
Akhmatova maintained at best a marginal existence, supported by the meager income of husbands and various benefactors, and later by working as a translator of other, lesser
poets' work into Russian, at the same time she became a
famous poet in the Soviet Union. Only with the easing of
restrictions on cultural life introduced by premier Nikita
Khrushchev beginning in the late 1950s was Akhmatova able
again to publish serious poetry.
     Akhmatova is known as Soviet Russia's greatest poet of
memory. In this poem written in 1929, she recalls the pre-
Soviet Petersburg:

This city, beloved by me since childhood,
Seemed to me today
In its December silence
Like my squandered inheritance.

Everything that came so easily,
That was so easy to give away:
Burning emotions, the sound of prayers,
And the blessing of the first song—

Everything flew off like transparent smoke,
Decayed in the depths of mirrors ...
And then a noiseless fiddler began to play
About the irrevocable.

But with a stranger's curiosity,
Captivated by each novelty,
I watched how the sleds skimmed,
And listened to my native tongue.

Then with a freshness wild and strong,
Happiness fanned my face,
As if an old dear friend
Had just stepped onto the porch with me.
  (Akhmatova 375–376)

Two of Akhmatova's most impressive longer poems are literary monuments to the great difficulties faced by people in the USSR during its darkest hours. The poem cycle "Requiem," written between 1935 and 1940, though published only in 1963, treats the Great Purges of the 1930s, in which several million innocent victims were executed by the state or sentenced to long terms in prison camps in which many died. Akhmatova's own son, Lev Gumilev, was arrested several times, guilty of nothing more than being the son of people the regime considered to be ideological opponents, and in 1938 he was given a ten-year sentence of hard labor in the far north of Russia. (Akhmatova's former husband Nikolai Gumilev had been executed in 1921 by the Soviet regime, which accused him of being a counter-revolutionary.) Akhmatova now joined the long lines of petitioners at Petersburg's prisons and offices of the NKVD, hoping to get a package to their arrested relative or perhaps a bit of information about his or her whereabouts.[9] At the beginning of the cycle Akhmatova includes these words:

> In the terrible years of the Yezhov terror [Egor Yezhov was the NKVD chief—BDW], I spent seventeen months in the prison lines of Leningrad. Once, someone "recognized" me. Then a woman with bluish lips standing behind me, who of course, had never heard me called by my name before, woke up from the stupor to which everyone had succumbed and whispered in my ear (everyone spoke in whispers there):
> "Can you describe this?"
> And I answered: "Yes, I can."
> Then something that looked like a smile passed over what had once been her face. (Akhmatova 384)

One of the most moving sections of the poem cycle describes the women waiting in these monstrous lines:

> I learned how faces fall,
> How terror darts from under eyelids,
> How suffering traces lines
> Of stiff cuneiform on cheeks,
> How locks of ashen-blonde or black
> Turn silver suddenly,
> Smiles fade on submissive lips
> And fear trembles in a dry laugh.
> And I pray not for myself alone,
> But for all those who stood with me
> In cruel cold, and in July's heat,
> At that blind, red wall.[10]

Akhmatova's other great lengthy work is "Poem Without a Hero," written between 1940 and 1962. Some 800-lines long and consisting of several parts, this complex poem is at heart a "suite of impressions," to use Victor Terras's phrase, from Akhmatova's own life and from the literary, theater, and musical scene of Petersburg just prior to World War I. (Terras 558) The poem is complex, with numerous literary and historical references and often obscure allusions. Blok and his poetry play an important role in the work, as do references to Pushkin. Akhmatova dedicated the entire poem to the victims of the 900-day blockade of Leningrad by the German armed forces from 1941 to 1944, in which over 600,000 people died of starvation and disease. In the poem's epilogue, Akhmatova addresses Leningrad directly:

> And not becoming my grave,
>   You, granite, infernal, dear to me,
>   Grew pale, benumbed and still.
> Our separation is imaginary:
>   We are inseparable,
>   My shadow is on your walls,
> My reflection in your canals,
>   The sound of my footsteps in the Hermitage halls
>   Where my friend walked with me,
> And in the ancient Volkov Field
>   Where I can freely weep
>   Over the silence of common graves.
> Everything recounted in Part One
>   About love, betrayal and passion,
>   Free verse flung from its wings,
> And my city stands, mended ...
>   Heavy are the gravestones
>   On your sleepless eyes.
> It seemed you were pursuing me,
>   You, who stayed to perish there
>   In the glitter of spires, in the shimmer of waters.
>   (Akhmatova 575)

The writer and critic Solomon Volkov, who was acquainted with Akhmatova during his youth in Leningrad, has written that Akhmatova's *Poem Without a Hero*, together with Pushkin's *The Bronze Horseman*, form a creative and historical arc along which the literary myth of Petersburg has been created. Highlighting a couplet from Part One of the poem (the subtitle of which is "a Petersburg Tale"), Volkov writes with insight on Akhmatova's view of history, her contribution to the mythic image of the city, and the role of poets in creating myth:

> For me the essence of Akhmatova's philosophy of history and her ideas on the evolution of the Petersburg mythos are most succinctly expressed in the lines, "Just as the future ripens in the past,/So the past smoulders in the future." This formula came to Akhmatova from her own experiences and therefore has a convincing ring. The role of "history's lighting rod" almost always falls on the poet. Though historical epochs mirror one another, the terrible predictability is visible only to the poet, whose role is to create all-encompassing historical myths. (Volkov, *St. Petersburg* 476)

In the poem "The Summer Garden," written late in her life, in 1959, Akhmatova evokes several historical periods in the history of Petersburg, while focusing immediate attention on the city's most famous park. Bordered by the Neva, the Fontanka, the Moika, and yet a fourth, smaller, canal, the Summer Garden was created by order of Peter the Great in the early 1700s and then rebuilt by Catherine the Great later in the century. It is filled with classical statues, and along the Neva embankment it is guarded by a stunning, wrought-iron fence.

> I want to visit the roses in that unique garden,
> Fenced by the world's most magnificent fence,
>
> Where the statues remember me as young,
> And I remember them under the Neva's waters.

In the fragrant silence among majestic linden trees,
I imagine the creaking of masts of ships.

And the swan, as before, floats across centuries,
Admiring the beauty of its twin.

And sleeping there, like the dead, are hundreds of
    thousands of footsteps
Of friends and enemies, enemies and friends.

And the procession of shades is endless,
From the granite vase to the door of the palace.

And everything glows like jasper and mother-of-pearl,
But the source of the light is mysteriously veiled.
    (Akhmatova 477)

Akhmatova saw several volumes of her poetry published in the post-World War II Soviet Union, in 1958 and 1961, albeit in censored form. She was also permitted to travel abroad several times; she received a literary prize in Italy in 1964, and in 1965, the year before her death, she was awarded an honorary doctorate at Oxford University. In the last years of her life she was mentor to a number of young Leningrad poets, most notable among them Joseph Brodsky.

While there is no museum to Mandelstam in Petersburg, there is an Akhmatova Museum. Facing the banks of the Fontanka River, just north of Nevsky Prospect, sits the yellow Sheremetev Palace, in the rear of which the Akhmatova Museum is located. (The best access to the museum is not along the Fontanka, but through the courtyard of 35 Liteiny Prospect.) Throughout her tempestuous and often tragic personal life, Akhmatova spend many years in a small apartment in this building, known in the Soviet era as the "Fountain House," after the river on whose banks it stands. Soon after the 1917 Revolution, the building was seized by the Soviet state and divided into communal apartments, a fate suffered by many of Petersburg's beautiful buildings. A noteworthy feature of the Akhmatova Museum is a portrait of the poet by Modigliani made in Paris in 1911.

JOSEPH BRODSKY

Petersburg is of key importance in the poetry of the sole native of the city to receive the Nobel Prize for Literature—Joseph Brodsky (1940–1996). Brodsky received the award in 1987, fifteen years after his deportation from the Soviet Union. In the Soviet Union his name could not be mentioned in public, but his fame only grew, as his poems were passed from reader to reader in *samizdat*. Solomon Volkov, who knew Brodsky both in Leningrad and in New York City, where Brodsky lived as an exile, writes: "The youth of Leningrad, seeking new paths, came

The 900-Day Siege of Leningrad—A Monument

An impressive monument on Victory Square (*Plosnchad Pobedy*) commemorates the struggle citizens of Leningrad endured during the Second World War when the city was under siege for 900 days by Nazi troops. Almost 600,000 residents died during the time of the siege—mostly of starvation, exposure, and bombardment, as all transport in and out of the city was cut off for close to three years.

The monument, on the main road to St. Petersburg's international Pulkovo Airport, is built in the shape of a massive broken ring representing all efforts to break the 900-day Siege. Visible from some distance, dark figures of mourning—tall sculptures of soldiers, sailors, and civilians—contrast with the light stone.

Lit with gas torches, the inside of the ring's walls are covered with engravings that depict scenes of courage demonstrated by the defenders of Leningrad. An exhibition about the Siege is located in a museum inside the monument.

into contact with the Petersburg mythos through Brodsky's poetry.... Many sought in his poems the key to the 'secret garden' of the old Petersburg culture, vanished, some thought, forever." (Volkov, *St. Petersburg* 518)

In his childhood, Brodsky lived on Liteiny Prospect in central Leningrad—by remarkable coincidence, in a small apartment in the aforementioned "Muruzy House." Even more amazingly, the room and a half Brodsky shared with his parents was carved out of the larger apartment that Merezhovsky and Gippius themselves had occupied.[11]

As a young man Brodsky became acquainted with Leningrad's working-class city outskirts. At age fifteen he abandoned school and soon took up work as a milling machine operator in a military arms factory. He later recalled:

The whole thing would have looked very absurd if it were not for those very early mornings when, having washed my breakfast down with pale tea, I would run to catch the streetcar and, adding my berry to the dark-gray bunch of human grapes hanging on the footboard, would sail though the pinkish-blue, watercolor-like city to the wooden doghouse of my factory's entrance. It had two guards checking our badges and its façade was decorated with classical veneered pilasters. I've noticed that the entrances of prisons, mental hospitals, and concentration camps are done in the same style: they all bear a hint of classistic or baroque porticoes. Quite an echo. Inside my shop, nuances of gray were interwoven under the ceiling, and the pneumatic hoses hissed quietly on the floor among the mazout puddles glittering with all the colors of the rainbow. By ten o'clock this metal jungle was in full swing, screeching and roaring, and the steel barrel of a would-be antiaircraft gun soared into the air like the disjointed neck of a giraffe. (*Less than One* 15–16)

As Brodsky considered Leningrad in his poetry (he preferred the popular, informal name *Piter*) he found the living, imperial city not amid its architectural riches, but instead in the hulking, crumbling apartment hi-rises and bleak industrial wastelands of the suburbs where he worked as a youth. This is clear from the opening lines of one his early poems, "From the Outskirts to the Center":

> Here I have visited anew
> this location of love, peninsula of mills,
> paradise of workshops and arcadia of factories.
> river heaven of steamships,
> again I whispered:
> here again I am among the young Lares.
> Here I have again run by the Little Okhta through
> a thousand arches.[12]

Brodsky's juxtaposition of the Soviet Union of the 1960s and 1970s with the classical world may seem at first unlikely. The more one reads Brodsky, however, the more impressive is the seriousness of his modernist dedication to understanding civilization and making his own contribution to it, not unlike the aims set out by the Acmeist poets earlier in the century. Brodsky's art entailed a return to the source waters of Western civilization—classical Greece and Rome.

While Leningrad was no longer the Alexandria it had been under the tsars, it remained a city whose glories were just possibly not relegated to the past. For Brodsky, Leningrad was a window on the world. Though it was a window certainly far less transparent than the one Peter had intended for the residents of his city, Brodsky with his intelligence and sensitivity was still able to use it to explore the path to more profound realms. Brodsky later elaborated on the attraction the Leningrad suburbs held for him:

> ... I realized that the outskirts were the beginning of the world, not the end. They were the end of the familiar world but the beginning of the unfamiliar world, which is much

bigger, much vaster. In principle the idea was that, in leaving
for the outskirts, you're distancing yourself from everything
you know and setting out for the real world. (Volkov, *Conversations with Joseph Brodsky* 21)

The Soviet regime and its imposed mores and ways of
thought were far too easy targets for Brodsky. Sifting through
time and place for the "real world" was what occupied Brodsky's
attention, as is evident in his early poem "A Halt in the Desert."
Here are the poem's beginning and final lines:

So few Greeks live in Leningrad today
that we have razed a Greek church, to make space
for a new concert hall, built in today's
grim and unhappy style. And yet a concert hall with more than fifteen hundred seats
is not so grim a thing. And who's to blame
if virtuosity has more appeal
than the worn banners of an ancient faith?
...
Tonight I stare out through the blank window
and think about that point to which we've come,
and then I ask myself: from which are we
now more remote—the world of ancient Greece,
or Orthodoxy? Which is closer now?
What lies ahead? Does a new epoch wait
for us? And, if it does, what duty do we owe?—
What sacrifices must we make for it? (Brodsky,
    Selected Poems 131–133)

For his unwillingness to accept the Soviet Union as the
center of the universe and the Communist Party as the safe-
guard of truth, or at least to keep silent about his doubts and
own convictions, the arch-conservative Leningrad Communist
Party officials put the twenty-three-old poet on trial in 1964 for
"malicious parasitism," that is, not holding a paid job, a crime

in Soviet law. A journalist at the trial recorded how Brodsky tried to explain to the judge that his work was that of poet:

> *Judge:* And who recognized that you are a poet? Who listed you among poets?
> *Brodsky:* No one. (Dispassionately.) Who listed me a member of the human race?
> *Judge:* Did you study this?
> *Brodsky:* What?
> *Judge:* To be a poet? Did you try to graduate from a school where they prepare ... where they teach ...
> *Brodsky:* I don't think that it comes from education.
> *Judge:* What then?
> *Brodsky:* I think that it's ... (bewildered) ... from God.
> (Volkov, *St. Petersburg* 477)

After a forced stay in a psychiatric hospital, Brodsky was sentenced to five years of forced labor in a remote area of northern Russia. He was released after a year and eight months; his case may have been helped by a private letter from Sartre to Supreme Soviet Chairman Anastas Mikoyan appealing for his release primarily on the grounds that Soviet sympathizers, like Sartre, were beginning to look bad because of how the poet was being treated. (Volkov, *St. Petersburg* 509–510) In 1972, Brodsky was forced to emigrate to the West, and he settled in New York City. Like another writer born in Petersburg, Vladimir Nabokov, Brodsky made the transition to English, in which he wrote both poems and essays.

Currently, there is an effort to turn a portion of the Muruzy House into a museum to Brodsky. For more information, see *http://brodsky.spb.ru/*.

NOTES

1. W. Bruce Lincoln, *Sunlight at Midnight: St. Petersburg and the Rise of Modern Russia* (New York, 2000), p. 130. The information in this paragraph is greatly informed by Lincoln's descriptions of Nevsky Prospect.

2. For details on addresses of locales in *Crime and Punishment* I am indebted to Kholshevnikov. Photographs of some of the locales of the novel in the Haymarket area can be seen on the Internet at *www.faculty.virgnia.edu/dostoevsky/texts/crime_and_punishment.html.*

3. Translator's note: A member of a dissenting religious sect which practiced castration. Many of the *Skoptsy* were money changers.

4. Translators' note: In the nineteenth century many merchants were peasants who had earned their fortunes in trade or were descended from such peasants. "Hereditary burgess" is an approximate translation of one of the legal class designations intended to confirm and formalize the merchant's acquired rank.

5. Cited in Solomon Volkov, *St. Petersburg: A Cultural History.* Translated by Antonina W. Bouis. (New York: The Free Press, 1995), p. 127. Merezhkovsky's treatise was published the next year in booklet form under the same title.

6. Cited in M.G. Kachurin, et al., ed. *Sankt-Peterburg v russkoi literatura*, Vol. 2 (St. Petersburg: Svet, 1996), p. 75. Translation by Bradley D. Woodworth.

7. Cited in Kachurin, et al., *Sankt-Peterburg v russkoi literature*, Vol. 2, p. 77. Translation by Bradley D. Woodworth.

8. Cited in Kachurin, et al., *Sankt-Peterburg v russkoi literature*, p. 183.

9. A fictional treatment of the experience of a Leningrad mother whose son is unjustly arrested in the

Purges can be found in Lydia Chukovskaya's, *Sofia Petrovna*. Translated by Aline Werth and Emended by Eliza Kellogg Klose (Evanston, IL.: Northwestern University Press, 1988).

10. *The Complete Poems of Anna Akhmatova*, p. 392. Lev Gumilev was arrested again in 1949 and released only in 1956.

11. Brodsky, *Less Than One: Selected Essays*, p. 452. In the essay "In a Room and a Half" Brodsky evocatively describes life in a Petersburg communal apartment.

12. Translation by Bradley D. Woodworth. The "Little Okhta" is a reference both to a river in the outskirts of Leningrad and to a nearby chemical factory that also bore the name "Okhta."

St. Petersburg is easily divided into the neighborhoods around and just beyond Nevsky Prospect, the city's most famous thoroughfare; the vicinity of Palace Square, which houses the grand Hermitage as well as a number of other museums and monuments; Vasilievsky Island; and the Petrograd side of the Neva River.

ON AND AROUND NEVKSY PROSPECT

Nevsky Prospect

St. Petersburg's Champs Elysée has been immortalized by countless Russian writers. In the early days of St. Petersburg's existence, it was simply the beginning of the road to the ancient city of Novgorod. But soon the street grew into an area of concentrated shopping, culture, and living.

Being the main street to run East-West from one meandering curve of the Neva River to another, this main shopping street also encompasses churches, museums, educational institutions, grocery stores, boutiques, perfumeries, galleries, book stores and everything else that constitutes the heart of a city.

Beginning at the far end of Nevsky on the banks of the Neva River, the Alexander Nevsky Lavra, a monastery founded by Peter the Great in 1710, anchors the boulevard to the East. Nevsky Prospect ends at the Admiralteistvo, on the northwestern side of the inner city area.

This is the densest area of St. Petersburg, where history, art, music, faith, celebration and present day life collide in one menagerie of 21st century Russia.

ALEXANDER NEVSKY MONASTERY

1 Pl. Alexandra Nevskogo • Tel: 812-274-1702

This monastery was named in honor of Prince Alexander Nevsky of Novgorod, who hindered Sweden and Germany's forward encroachment on Russian territory in the 1200s. Peter the Great founded and dedicated the monastery to Nevsky in 1710.

The Lazarus and the Tikhvin cemeteries on the grounds contain the tombs of literary and musical luminaries such as Rimsky-Korsakov, Mussorsky, Borodin, and Tchaikovksy. Churches, a museum, and monuments, are also located at the Monastery.

INSURRECTION SQUARE

Nevsky pr.

The site of many uprisings over the centuries, this busy square with an obelisk at its center is just across from the Moscow Railroad Station. A metro station of the same name is just across the street, making this a busy intersection with several main roads leading into and through the square.

PALACE OF PRINCE BELOSELSKY-BELOZERSKY

41 Nevsky pr. • Tel: 812-315-5236

This neo-baroque confection, which during the Soviet era was painted a fire engine red, housed the local Communist Party headquarters. Now a more muted peach, the building serves as a hub for exhibitions and concerts. Designed by Stackenschneider in 1848, its interior doesn't quite hold up to its ornate façade, but is still worth a look, with the views across the Fontanka River and Nevsky Prospect.

ANICHKOV BRIDGE

Nevsky pr.

At one time this bridge, spanning the Fontanka River, marked the city limits of St. Petersburg. Named after Colonel Mikhail

Anichkov, who built the first bridge here with his troops in the early 1800s, it is an impressive sight with its massive four bronze horse sculptures designed by Peter Klodt. These were put up in 1941 at the four corners of the Anichkov bridge, but taken down and buried during World War II. After victory in 1945, they went back to their rightful place of guarding over those who come in and out of the city.

ANICHKOV PALACE

Nevksy pr.

Designed by Mikhail Zemtsov and completed by the Italian architect Rastrelli, this striking building was commissioned by Empress Elizabeth for her lover Alexei Razumovsky in the mid-1700s. Catherine the Great later gifted the palace to her lover Grigory Potemkin, the one responsible for the concept of "Potemkin villages," when he collaborated to have quickly-assembled facades of pleasant looking villages erected as Catherine toured the impoverished Russian countryside.

YELISEYEV FOOD EMPORIUM

56 Nevsky pr. • Tel: 812-314-2401

An ornate food hall built at the turn of the century for the merchant Yeliseyev to ply his imported delicacies. The architecture, inside and out, is an ode to glorious undulating art nouveau, with gilded floral decorative ornamentation on the walls and ceiling, stained glass windows, and massive chandeliers.

STROGANOV PALACE

17 Nevsky pr. • Tel: 812-311-2360

Built for the prominent Stroganov family between 1752 and 1754 by the royal architect Francesco-Bartholomeo Rastrelli, (who also designed the Winter Palace and Smolny Cathedral), the palace is now part of the Russian State Museum and houses a collection of

Russian icons from the Stroganov family, as well as a wax museum. The wax figures are dedicated to the Romanov Dynasty.

DOSTOEVKSY LITERARY-MEMORIAL MUSEUM

5/2 Kuznechny per. • Tel: 812-311-4031

Fyodor Dostoevsky lived an apartment in this building, from 1878 to 1881, as he wrote *The Brothers Karamazov*. The author, known for depictions of a dark and mysterious St. Petersburg populated by curious characters, preferred writing in an area and around the type of people who might figure in his novels.

ANNA AKHMATOVA MUSEUM

34 nab. Fontanka • Tel: 812-272-2211

One of Russia's favorite poets, Anna Akhmatova lived in a communal apartment during the Soviet era in this former palace of Count Sheremetyev. Exhibitions, poetry readings and events are scheduled here.

PASSAGE TRADING HOUSE

48 Nevsky pr. • Tel: 812-571-7084

Hours: Monday through Saturday 10.00 A.M. to 9.00 P.M., Sundays 11.00 A.M. to 9.00 P.M.
This shopping arcade, an early ornate version of an interior mall, with three stories and balconies overlooking a main glass-domed hall, now houses clothing boutiques, Italian shoe stores, and souvenir shops.

CHURCH OF THE SAVIOR ON SPILLED BLOOD

Nab. kanala Griboyedov

This splendid onion-domed church was built on the spot where Emperor Alexander II was assassinated by revolutionaries in March 1881. The church was built between 1883 and 1907 as the

Resurrection of Christ Church or the Church of Our Savior on Spilled Blood, and contains numerous colorful mosaics, inside and out. The church was designed and decorated by the famous Russian artists Vasnetsov, Nesterov, and Vrubel.

DOM KNIGI (HOUSE OF BOOKS)

28 Nevsky pr. • Tel: 812-219-6402

Housed in the pre-revolutionary offices of the Singer Sewing Machine Company, Dom Knigi maintained several floors of books, posters, calendars, postcards, and every other imaginable printed material, during the Soviet Era. The striking golden globe in a dome on the top of the building is an unforgettable landmark on Nevsky Prospekt. Today it is under reconstruction and will still maintain a book shop as well as other commercial ventures.

LITERARY CAFE

18 Nevsky pr. • Tel: 812-312-6057

Famed as the site of Alexander Pushkin's last meal before his ill-fated duel, the literary cafe—once a grand salon with cavern-like arched ceilings, fine china and chandeliers, even into the 1990s—has now shrunk into a second-floor dining room overlooking the picturesque Moika Canal.

BANK BRIDGE

Kanal Griboedov

This charming footbridge is memorable for its glorious gilt-winged griffons, said to guard the treasures of the state bank, which was formerly located in a neighboring building.

LION BRIDGE

Kanal Griboedov

When it opened in July 1826, Lion Bridge was an innovation, because its support was hidden in the metal bodies of the four white cast-iron lions which stand in majestic pairs at each end of the bridge.

KAZAN CATHEDRAL

2 Kazansky Pl. • Tel: 812-314-4663

Constructed between 1801 and 1811 by the architect Voronikhin, the cathedral, with its grand stone colonnades, was inspired by the Basilica of St. Peter's in Rome and was intended to become the country's main Orthodox Church. After the war of 1812 and the defeat of Napoleon, the church became a monument to Russian victory. Field Marshal Mikhail Kutuzov, honored for winning that campaign, was buried inside the church.

When the Bolsheviks came to power the cathedral was closed in 1929, and instead served as the Museum of the History of Religion and Atheism. During Gorbachev's years of perestroika, the small park in front of the cathedral and the cathedral's wide exterior ledges themselves became a stage for musicians and impromptu youthful gatherings. The cathedral once again holds religious services.

THE ADMIRALTY

Admiralteysky pr.

Nevsky Prospekt ends at this Russian Empire-style structure that was originally designed to be a dockyard. Some of the first ships of Russia's Baltic fleet were built here. The Admiralty's gilded spire is a landmark visible from a number of central streets. It was Russia's Naval Headquarters until 1917, and now serves as a naval college.

SQUARE OF THE ARTS

Just off Nevksy Prospect, past the elegant façade of the Grand Hotel Europe, a pedestrian area of gardens, parks and courtyards lead to some of Russia's most important museums and historic structures.

SUMMER GARDEN

Dvortsovaya nab.

The Summer Garden is an old park that witnessed the most spectacular moments of St Petersburg's early history. In 1704 Peter the Great founded his summer residence in a new capital—the Summer Palace. The Park around it was laid out in French style and decorated with marble Italian Baroque sculptures. They are covered with wooden lock boxes in the winter to protect them from the cold.

GRAND HOTEL EUROPE

1/7 Mikhailovkaya ul. • Tel: 812-329-6000
www.grand-hotel-europe.com

This beautiful structure appeared in the 1820s and later appeared as the Cuolon Hotel in 1830. It was integrated with neighboring houses by Carlo Rossi by means of the neoclassical façade that covered the existing buildings, later becoming the Hotel de l'Europe in 1875. At the turn of the century the Swedish-Russian architect, Fyodor Lidval, redesigned much of the hotel's interior, adding Art Nouveau features. During the First World War and the Bolshevik Revolution, the building served alternately as a hospital, orphanage, and offices. It was finally restored in 1989.

STATE RUSSIAN MUSEUM

4/2 Inzhenernaya ul. • Tel: 812-595-4248
www.rusmuseum.ru

Housing one of the best and most comprehensive collections of Russian art in the world, the State Russian Museum is now composed of seven structures around the city, the main building being the former Mikhailov Palace. Originally called the "Russian Museum of Emperor Alexander III," this collection was established in 1895, with donations from the Hermitage, the Academy of Fine Arts, and royal palaces surrounding St. Petersburg.

The collection includes grand works by famous Russian artists over the centuries, from iconographers, to Ilya Repin, Mikhail Vrubel, Serov, to 20th century works by Kandinsky and Malevich.

THE MARBLE PALACE

5/1 Millionaya ul. • Tel: 812-312-9196

Commissioned by Empress Catherine the Great for Grigory Orlov, the palace was designed and built between 1768 and 1785 by the Italian-born architect Antonio Rinaldi. It was originally decorated with 32 different types of marble. Today it houses the Russian Museum's new modern and pop art collections.

PALACE SQUARE AND ITS SURROUNDINGS

PALACE SQUARE

A square on the grandest scale, surrounded by some of Russia's most incredible architecture—the Hermitage and the palatial General Staff Building—from which imperial Russia was ruled from for over 200 years. It also was the place of revolt and revolution, during Bloody Sunday of 1905, when imperial troops opened fire on peaceful demonstrators; and again in 1917, when Bolshevik revolutionaries stormed the Winter Palace to overthrow the provisional government.

The Alexander Column stands tall at the center of the square, commemorating Russia's victory over Napoleon. Carved from a single piece of granite, the column stands on its own with no form of attachment to the base.

THE HERMITAGE MUSEUM

Dvortsovaya nab. 32-28 • Tel: 812-710-9625
www.hermitagemuseum.org

Hours: Tuesday-Saturday 10:30A.M.–6:00P.M., Sundays and national holidays 10:30A.M.–5:00P.M.
The State Hermitage occupies six magnificent buildings along the embankment of the Neva River. The Winter Palace, the former residence of Russian tsars that was designed by Francesco Bartolomeo Rastrelli, constitutes the main structure of the museum. The Hermitage collections number over 3 million works of art spanning from the Stone Age to the 20th century.

THE WINTER PALACE

From the 1760s onwards the Winter Palace was the main residence of the Russian Tsars. The Baroque-style teal-hued palace boasts 1,786 doors, 1,945 windows and 1,057 halls and rooms. The Winter Palace was built between 1754 and 1762 for Empress Elizabeth, the daughter of Peter the Great. She died before the palace's completion, but Catherine the Great oversaw the final work and started the collection that would become the State Hermitage Museum.

GENERAL STAFF BUILDING

Dvortsovaya Pl.

A great arched building that spans the eastern side of Palace Square, this served as the army headquarters, as well as the Ministry of Foreign Affairs and Finance under tsarist rule. It was designed by Italian architect Carlo Rossi between 1819 and 1829 in a neoclassical style.

ALEXANDER PUSHKIN APARTMENT MUSEUM

12 nab. Moika • Tel: 812-311-3531
www.museumpushkin.ru

This literary museum, dedicated to Russia's most celebrated poet, stands just a few meters away from Palace Square on the quiet embankment of the Moika River. The museum is housed in Alexander Pushkin's memorial apartment where he lived between 1836 and 1837, and died after being wounded in duel for his wife's honor. The museum boasts numerous literary and historical exhibitions, charting his life, work and times.

AROUND THE ADMIRALTY

ALEXANDER GARDEN

The Alexander Garden, near the Admiralty, was planted and named after Emperor Alexander. It was once used for military exercises and public celebrations. A path leads to the famous Bronze Horseman monument to Peter I, described by Pushkin in his eponymous poem.

THE BRONZE HORSEMAN

Alexander Gardens

Constructed at the request of Catherine the Great to honor the founder of St. Petersburg, the equestrian statue depicts Peter the Great as a Roman hero. The pedestal is made of a single piece of red granite molded into the shape of a cliff. Peter is shown on the horse charging ahead, leading Russia forward.

ST. ISAAC'S CATHEDRAL

1 Isaakievskaya Pl. • Tel: 812-315-9732

Originally the city's main church, St. Isaac's was built between 1818 and 1858 by a French-born architect to be the largest cathedral in Russia. The cathedral's exterior is decorated with sculptures and majestic granite columns, made of single pieces of red granite. Inside, detailed mosaics, icons, paintings, and columns made of malachite and lapis lazuli adorn the church which was designed to accommodate 14,000 standing worshipers. During the Soviet era the church was closed and used as a museum. Today, services are held on special holidays.

MARIINSKY THEATER OF OPERA AND BALLET

Teatralnaya Pl. 1 • Tel: 812-326-4141
www.mariinsky.ru

This striking powder-blue structure, dating back to 1859, originally housed another theater but was remodeled and taken over by the famed Mariinsky company, (later called the Kirov in the Soviet era). In pre-revolutionary Russia the theater hosted singers, such as Fyodor Shaliapin, and dancers like Vatslav Nizhinsky and Anna Pavlova. The ballet troupe also cultivated such modern ballet greats as Rudolph Nureyev and Mikhail Baryshnikov. Today, acclaimed maestro Valeri Gergiev oversees the orchestra and opera.

YUSUPOV PALACE

94 nab. Moika • Tel: 812-314-9883

On the Moika River stands the bright yellow residence of the wealthy Yusupov family. The palace is most renowned for being the place of the murder of Grigory Rasputin. In 1916, a group of the city's noble elite, including a grand dukes and Prince Felix Yusupov, conspired to kill Rasputin, a monk of sorts who influenced decisions of the royal family. Rasputin was murdered at the Yusupov Palace on the night of December 16, 1916.

VASILIEVKSY ISLAND

Vasilievsky Island is the largest island in the Neva delta. A number of its architectural monuments date to the 19th century, during a time of growth and trade, as witnessed by the Customs House and the Stock Exchange, now a naval museum. These, and the majority of significant structures on Vasiliesvsky, are built on the Strelka (the spit) of the eastern side of the island. St. Petersburg State

University, the Academy of Arts, and a number of other museums line the eastern side of the island.

THE STOCK EXCHANGE /NAVAL MUSEUM

4 Birzhevaya Pl. • Tel: 812-328-2502

Hours: Wednesday–Sunday 10:30A.M.–8P.M.
Modeled after a Greek temple, the Birzha, or Stock Exchange, was constructed in the early 1800s. By 1940, the building also housed the Naval Museum displaying Russia's naval history, as well as models of ships built in Russia's naval yards since Peter the Great's reign. Modern-day naval exhibits include submarines and missiles. Two sepia-colored Rostral Columns, used as navigational beacons in the 1800s, stand guard.

KUNSTKAMMER

3 Universitetskaya nab. • Tel: 812-328-1412

Hours: Friday–Wednesday, 11:00A.M.–6:00P.M.
Known as the Chamber of Arts, or Curiosities, the baroque-style building housed Peter the Great's sometimes-gruesome collection of human and animal organs and fetuses preserved in jars, as well as jewels, stones, and trinkets. The building today also houses the Museum of Anthropology and Ethnography.

MENSHIKOV PALACE

15 Universitetskaya nab. • Tel: 812-323-1112

Hours: Tuesday–Sunday, 10:30A.M.–4:30P.M.
Alexander Menshikov (1673-1729), friend of Peter the Great, was promoted to the position of a duke and the Governor General of St. Petersburg in the early 1700s. It was under his supervision that the Peter and Paul Fortress, as well as the fort of Kronstadt in the Gulf of Finland, were built. His palace was one of the most ornate in the city. Menshikov effectively ruled the country as he was overseeing the passage of the throne from Peter the Great to his wife Catherine I after Peter's death in 1725. The palace has belonged to the Hermitage since 1967.

REPIN INSTITUTE OF PAINTING, SCULPTURE, AND ARCHITECTURE (ST. PETERSBURG ACADEMY OF ARTS)

17 Universitetskaya nab. • Tel: 812-323-6496

One of the most renowned institutes for the fine arts, the Repin Institute, or Academy of Art, as it is alternatively called, was founded by Peter the Great to influence Russian art by Western standards of instruction. Catherine the Great continued to cultivate the school, giving it the moniker of "academy" during her reign. The building, flanked by two great sphinx statues, is home to vaulted hallways, studios and classrooms unchanged in centuries, in which students are instructed in drawing, painting, sculpture, and iconography. A grand hall for lectures and exhibitions is open to students and visitors.

PETER AND PAUL FORTRESS

Zayachy Ostrov

The impressive fort, with a gleaming golden spire, stands on the delta of the Neva River. The fortress was built when Peter the Great reclaimed the lands along the Neva River from the Swedes in 1703 to create St. Petersburg. Composed of many buildings and squares within a fortress wall, the Peter and Paul Fortress housed part of the city's garrison and jail from 1721 on. No common prison, the jail housed political prisoners as well—including Peter's own rebellious son Alexei, and later Dostoyevsky, Gorky, Trotsky and Lenin's older brother, Alexander. The Peter and Paul Cathedral, the burial place of all the Russian Emperors and Empresses from Peter the Great to Alexander III, stands in the middle of the fortress. On top of the cathedral's gilded spire a golden angel holds a cross. At 404 feet tall, the cathedral is the highest building in the city. Other buildings in the fortress include the City History Museum and the Mint.

PETROGRAD SIDE

This mostly residential side of St. Petersburg is remarkable for street upon street of charming turreted apartment houses. With influences drawn from simple Baltic, Scandinavian, and Prussian architecture, these neighborhoods always maintained a pleasant small-town atmosphere even during Soviet times. Only infrequently is the European architecture interrupted by heavy-handed, chunky Soviet-style buildings ... mostly further toward the outskirts of the city.

AVRORA

Petrovskaya nab.

The cruiser Aurora (Avrora in Russian) was built just before 1900 and joined Russia's Baltic fleet in 1903, taking part in the Russo-Japanese War of 1904–1905. But in 1917 it played its greatest role. On October 25, 1917, it fired a blank shot at the Winter Palace (then the residence of the Provisional Government), giving the signal to the rebellious workers, soldiers, and sailors of the city to storm the palace. That moment set in motion the events that would begin over 70 years of Communist leadership.

CHRONOLOGY

862   Varangian warrior Rurik establishes the dynasty of the Kievan Rus in Novgorod.

882   Oleg moves the Rus to Kiev.

988   Grand Duke Vladimir I converts to Russian Orthodoxy.

1169   Prince Oleg Bogolubsky moves capital to Vladimir, near Moscow.

1237–1240   The Mongols invade Russia conquering and destroying its main cities except Novgorod and Pskov. Tatars establish the empire of the Golden Horde in southern Russia.

1271   Moscow becomes the Grand Duchy of Suzdal-Vladimir.

1380   Dmitri Donskoi defeats the Tatars and becomes the Grand Duke of Moscow.

1462–1505   Ivan the III (the Great) annexes surrounding areas to build an autocratic state; religious leaders call Moscow the Third Rome, heir to Rome and Constantinople.

1552–1556   Ivan the Terrible conquers the Tatars of Kazan and Astrakhan, and establishes Russian rule over lower and middle Volga and begins annexation of Siberia.

1589   The Russian Orthodox Church becomes independent of other Orthodox churches.

1605   The Time of Troubles commences and Poland invades Russia.

1613   The national council elects Michael Romanov as tsar, beginning the Romanov dynasty.

1689–1725	Peter the Great introduces reforms, creates a conscript army and navy, creates new government structures, and establishes Russia's new capital, St. Petersburg.
1703	Construction on the Peter and Paul Fortress begins in St. Petersburg.
1704	Peter the Great's Summer Palace is constructed.
1749	Alexander Radishchev is born. He will write "Journey from St. Petersburg to Moscow."
1754	Construction begins on the St. Petersburg's Winter Palace for Empress Elizabeth; the design is by Rastrelli.
1762	Catherine the Great comes to power and pushes Russia to become a leading power in Europe.
1764	The Hermitage Museum is founded.
1772–1814	Russia acquires Crimea.
1776	The Bolshoi Ballet is founded.
1783	Catherine the Great founds the Mariinsky Theater.
1799	Alexander Pushkin is born.
1809	Nikolai Gogol is born.
1812	Napoleon invades Russia but is crushed by the Russian winter.
1817	Alexei Tolstoy is born.
1818	Construction begins on St. Petersburg's St. Isaac's Cathedral.
1828	Leo Tolstoy is born in Yasnaya Polyana.
1833	Alexander Pushkin writes "The Bronze Horseman."
1837	Alexander Pushkin is killed in a duel along a St. Petersburg canal.
1853–1857	The Crimean War.
1856-64	The Caucasian War completes annexation of the North Caucasus.

1864   Dostoevsky's "Notes from the Underground" is published.

1861   Alexander I emancipates the serfs.

1868   Maxim Gorky is born.

1877–1878   Russia goes to war with Turkey in the Russian-Turkish war.

1889   Poet Anna Akhmatova is born.

1890   Boris Pasternak is born.

1895   Satirist writer Mikhail Zoshchenko is born in Poltava.

1897   The Social Democratic Party is founded and in 1903 fractures into Bolshevik and Menshevik factions.

1899   Vladimir Nabokov is born.

1904–1905   Russia expands into Manchuria, which leads to war with Japan.

1905   Revolution forces Tsar Nicholas II to concede to a constitution and establish a parliament, called the Duma.

1914   Russia enters World War I.

1917   Workers and sailors capture government buildings and the Winter Palace in St. Petersburg when the Bolsheviks overthrow the provisional government of Alexander Kerensky.

Tsar Nicholas abdicates, ending the Romanov dynasty as Vladimir Ilych Lenin takes over to lead the new Russian Soviet Socialist Republic.

1918   The Bolsheviks assassinate Tsar Nicholas. Nabokov emigrates to England. Alexander Solzhenitsyn is born.

1918–1922   Civil war erupts in Russia.

1922   The Union of Soviet Socialist Republics is created and Zoshchenko publishes first collection of short stories.

1924 Joseph Stalin comes to power.

1933 Poet Yevgeny Yevtushenko is born.

1936–1938 Millions die in Stalin's purges.

1941 Nazi Germany invades the USSR.

1940 Nabokov moves to the Unites States from England. Joseph Brodsky is born.

1945 World War II ends and the USSR occupies Eastern Europe.

1946 An official decree bans Anna Akhmatova's poetry from being published.

1953 Stalin dies and Nikita Khrushchev takes power as first secretary of the Communist Party.

1956 Krushchev denounces Stalin.

1964 Leonid Brezhnev takes over as first secretary of the Communist Party.

1985 Mikhail Gorbachev comes to power and institutes new freedoms with glasnost and perestroika.

1991 The Soviet Union collapses and Boris Yeltsin becomes the first president of Russia.

1993 Russians approve a new constitution which gives the president sweeping powers, after a violent parliamentary rebellion.

1994 Russian troops invade breakaway republic of Chechnya.

1996 Yeltsin is reelected for another term.

2000 Vladimir Putin is elected president.

2003 St. Petersburg celebrates its 300th anniversary.

BIBLIOGRAPHY

Akhmatova, Anna. *The Complete Poems of Anna Akhmatova.* Expanded Edition. Translated by Judith Hemschemeyer. Edited and introduced by Robert Reeder. Boston: Zephyr Press, 1997.

Antsiferov, N. *Dusha Peterburga* [The Spirit of Petersburg]. Petersburg: Brokgauz-Efron, 1922.

Bater, James H. *St. Petersburg: Industrialization and Change.* Montreal: McGill-Queen's University Press, 1976.

Belov, S.V. *Peterburg Dostoevskogo.* St. Petersburg: Aleteia, 2002.

Bely, Andrei. *Petersburg.* Translated, annotated, and introduced by Robert A. Maguire and John E. Malmstad. Bloomington: Indiana University Press, 1978.

Berman, Marshall. *All That Is Solid Melts Into Air: The Experience of Modernity.* New York: Penguin Books, 1982.

Blok, Alexander. *The Twelve and Other Poems.* Translated from the Russian by Jon Stallworthy and Peter France. London: Eyre & Spottiswoode, 1970.

Brodsky, Joseph. *Less than One: Selected Essays.* New York: Farrar, Straus, Giroux; 1986.

———. *Selected Poems.* Translated and introduced by George L. Kline, with a foreword by W.H. Auden. Baltimore: Penguin Books, 1974.

Cracraft, James. *The Revolution of Peter the Great.* Cambridge, MA: Harvard University Press, 2003.

Dokusov, A.M., ed. *Literaturnye pamiatnye mesta Leningrada.* Leningrad: Lenizdat, 1976.

Dostoevsky, Fyodor. *The Adolescent.* Translated by Andrew R. MacAndrew. New York: Doubleday, 1971.

———. *Crime and Punishment.* Translated by Richard Pevear and Larissa Volokhonsky. New York: A.A. Knopf, 1993.

——. *The Idiot.* Translated by Henry and Olga Carlisle. New York: Signet, 1969.

——. *The Insulted and the Injured.* Translated by Constance Garnett. New York: Macmillan, 1923.

——. *Notes from Underground and the Grand Inquisitor.* Translated by Ralph E. Matlaw. New York: Meridian, 1991.

——. *A Writer's Diary,* Volume One 1873–1876. Translated and Annotated by Kenneth Lantz. Evanston, IL: Northwestern University Press, 1993.

Fanger, Donald. *Dostoevsky and Romantic Realism: A Study of Dostoevsky in Relation to Balzac, Dickens, and Gogol.* Chicago: University of Chicago Press, 1967.

Frank, Joseph. *Dostoevsky: Seeds of Revolt, 1821–1849.* Princeton: Princeton University Press, 1976.

George, Arthur L. with Elena George. *St. Petersburg: Russia's Window to the Future—The First Three Centuries.* Lanham, MD: Taylor Trade Publishing, 2003.

Gogol, Nikolai. *The Collected Tales of Nikolai Gogol,* Translated and annotated by Richard Pevear and Larissa Volokhonsky. New York: Vintage, 1998.

Hackel, Sergei. *The Poet and the Revolution: Aleksander Blok's 'The Twelve.'* Oxford: The Clarendon Press, 1975.

Hamm, Michael F., ed. *The City in Late Imperial Russia.* Bloomington: Indiana University Press, 1986.

Herzen, Alexander. *My Past and Thoughts: The Memoirs of Alexander Herzen.* Vol. 2. Translated by Constance Garnett. Revised by Humphrey Higgens. London: Chatto & Windus, 1968.

Hosking, Geoffrey. *Russia and the Russians: A History.* Harvard University Press: Cambridge, Mass., 2001.

Kisch, Cecil. *Alexander Blok: Prophet of Revolution.* London: Weidefeld and Nicolson, 1960.

Kovalchuk, V.M., et al., ed. *Sankt-Peterburg: 300 let istorii.* St. Petersburg: Nauka, 2003.

⬤ BIBLIOGRAPHY

Lincoln, W. Bruce. *Sunlight at Midnight: St. Petersburg and the Rise of Modern Russia.* New York: Basic Books, 2001

Mandelstam, Osip. *50 Poems.* Translated by Bernard Meares. New York: Persea Books, 1977.

———. *Complete Poetry of Osip Emilevich Mandelstam.* Translated by Burton Raffel and Alla Burago. With an introduction and notes by Sidney Monas. Albany: State University of New York Press, 1973.

———. *Poems from Mandelstam.* Translated by R.H. Morrison. Rutherford, NJ: Fairleigh Dickinson University Press, 1990.

Mickiewicz, Adam. *Poems by Adam Mickiewicz.* Translated by various hands and edited by George Rapall Noyes. New York: The Polish Institute of Arts and Sciences in America, 1944.

Mironov, Boris, with Ben Eklof, *The Social History of Imperial Russia, 1700–1917.* Volumes I and II. Boulder, CO.: Westview Press, 2000.

Nabokov, Vladimir. *Nikolai Gogol.* New York: New Directions, 1961.

———. *Speak, Memory: An Autobiography Revisited.* New York: Everyman's Library, 1999.

Pushkin, Alexander. *The Bronze Horseman: Selected Poems of Alexander Pushkin.* Translated and Introduced by D. M. Thomas. New York: Viking Press, 1982.

Schenker, Alexander M. *The Bronze Horseman: Falconet's Monument to Peter the Great.* New Haven: Yale University Press, 2003.

Schlögel, Karl. *Jenseits des Großen Oktober. Das Laboratorium der Moderne Petersburg 1909–1921.* Berlin: Hanser, 1998

Shangina, I.I. et al., ed. *Mnogonatsional'nyi Peterburg.* St. Petersburg: Iskusstvo-SPB, 2002.

Terras, Victor. *A History of Russian Literature.* New Haven: Yale University Press, 1991.

Volkov, Solomon. *Conversations with Joseph Brodsky: A Poet's Journey Through the Twentieth Century.* New York: The Free Press, 1998.

———. *St. Petersburg: A Cultural History.* Translated by Antonina W. Bouis. New York: The Free Press, 1995.

FURTHER READING

Follett, Ken. *The Man from St. Petersburg.* New York: Signet, 1998.

Dostoevsky, Fyodor. *Crime and Punishment.* New York: Bantam Classics. Reissue edition, 1984.

———. *The House of the Dead.* New York: Penguin Books. Reprint edition, 1986.

———. *Notes from Underground.* New York: Vintage Classics. Reprint edition, 1994.

George, Arthur and Elena George. *St. Petersburg: Russia's Window to the Future, The First Three Centuries.* Lanham, MD: Taylor Trade Publishing, 2003.

Giangrande, Cathy. *Saint Petersburg: Museums, Palaces, and Historic Collections.* Charlestown, MA: Bunker Hill Publishing, 2003.

Kokker, Steve and Nick Selby. *Lonely Planet St. Petersburg.* Oakland, CA: Lonely Planet Publications. 3rd edition, 2002.

Lincoln, Bruce. *Sunlight at Midnight: St. Petersburg and the Rise of Modern Russia.* New York: The Perseus Press, 2001.

Massie, Robert K. *Peter the Great.* New York: Ballantine Books. Reissue edition, 1981.

———. *Nicholas and Alexandra: The Story of the Love That Ended an Empire.* New York: Ballantine Books, 2005.

Massie, Suzanne. *Land of the Firebird.* New York: Simon & Schuster, 1981.

Orttung, Robert W. *From Leningrad to St. Petersburg.* New York: Palgrave Macmillan, 1995.

Ometev, Boris and John Stuart *St. Petersburg: Portrait of an Imperial City.* Vendome Press, 1990.

Richardson. Dan. *The Rough Guide To St. Petersburg.* New York: Rough Guides Limited. 5th edition. 2004.

Shvidkovsky, Dmitri. *St. Petersburg: Architecture of the Tsars.* New York: Abbeville Press, 1996.

Volkov, Solomon. *St. Petersburg: A Cultural History.* New York: The Free Press, 1995.

Sutcliffe, Mark, Frank Althaus, and Yury Molodkovets. *Petersburg Perspectives.* London: Booth-Clibborn, 2003.

Youssoupoff, Prince Felix. *Lost Splendor: The Amazing Memoirs of the Man Who Killed Rasputin.* New York: Helen Marx Books, 2003.

Zoshchenko, Mikhail. *Scenes from the Bath-house and Other Stories of Communist Russia.* Ann Arbor: University of Michigan Press. 1961.

———. *Nervous People and Other Satires.* Bloomington: Indiana University Press. 1975.

WEBSITES

Petersburg City / Guide to St. Petersburg
http://petersburgcity.com/

St. Petersburg / Leningrad
www.helsinki.fi/hum/slav/spb/project.htm

St. Petersburg, Russia
www.petersburg-russia.com/

The State Hermitage Museum
www.hermitagemuseum.org/

INDEX

PICTURE **CREDITS**

CONTRIBUTORS

HAROLD BLOOM is Sterling Professor of the Humanities at Yale University. He is the author of over 20 books, including *Shelley's Mythmaking* (1959), *The Visionary Company* (1961), *Blake's Apocalypse* (1963), *Yeats* (1970), *A Map of Misreading* (1975), *Kabbalah and Criticism* (1975), *Agon: Toward a Theory of Revisionism* (1982), *The American Religion* (1992), *The Western Canon* (1994), and *Omens of Millennium: The Gnosis of Angels, Dreams, and Resurrection* (1996). *The Anxiety of Influence* (1973) sets forth Professor Bloom's provocative theory of the literary relationships between the great writers and their predecessors. His most recent books include *Shakespeare: The Invention of the Human* (1998), a 1998 National Book Award finalist, *How to Read and Why* (2000), *Genius: A Mosaic of One Hundred Exemplary Creative Minds* (2002), *Hamlet: Poem Unlimited* (2003), and *Where Shall Wisdom be Found* (2004). In 1999, Professor Bloom received the prestigious American Academy of Arts and Letters Gold Medal for Criticism, and in 2002 he received the Catalonia International Prize.

BRADLEY D. WOODWORTH is a Research Affiliate in Yale University's History Department. He holds a Ph.D. in Russian History from Indiana University, and an M.A. in Russian and Soviet Studies from Harvard University. He completed a B.A. in Russian Language and Literature at Brigham Young University. He is the author of numerous articles on the history of the Russian empire and the Baltic provinces.

CONSTANCE E. RICHARDS is an author and journalist who lived in Russia for nearly seven years, writing for *Time Magazine, LIFE, Time-LIFE Books,* and *Moscow Magazine,* among other publications. She is the author/co-author of seven non-fiction books, including *Artful Asheville: Along the Urban Trail* and *Insiders' Guide: The North Carolina Mountains.* She specializes in travel writing and visual arts critique.